No More Science Kits or Texts in Isolation

DEAR READERS,

Much like the diet phenomenon *Eat This, Not That*, this series aims to replace some existing practices with approaches that are more effective—healthier, if you will—for our students. We hope to draw attention to practices that have little support in research or professional wisdom and offer alternatives that have greater support. Each text is collaboratively written by authors representing research and practice. Section 1 offers practitioners' perspectives on a practice in need of replacing and helps us understand the challenges, temptations, and misunderstandings that have led us to this ineffective approach. Section 2 provides a researcher's perspective on the lack of research to support the ineffective practice(s) and reviews research supporting better approaches. In Section 3, the authors representing practitioners' perspectives give detailed descriptions of how to implement these better practices. By the end of each book, you will understand both what not to do, and what to do, to improve student learning.

It takes courage to question one's own practice—to shift away from what you may have seen throughout your years in education and toward something new that you may have seen few if any colleagues use. We applaud you for demonstrating that courage and wish you the very best in your journey from this to that.

Best wishes,

—*Nell K. Duke and M. Colleen Cruz, series editors*

No More Science Kits or Texts in Isolation

Teaching Science and Literacy Together

JACQUELINE BARBER

GINA N. CERVETTI

HEINEMANN
Portsmouth, NH

Heinemann
361 Hanover Street
Portsmouth, NH 03801–3912
www.heinemann.com

Offices and agents throughout the world

The authors and publisher wish to thank those who have generously given permission to reprint borrowed material:

Text credits

Excerpt from the Common Core State Standards. Copyright © 2010 by the National Governors Association Center for Best Practices and Council of Chief State School Officers. All rights reserved.

Excerpt from "Science, language, and literacy: Learning to read, reading to learn" by Pamela J. Hines, Brad Wible, and Melissa McCartney from *Science*, Volume 328, Issue 5977, April 23, 2010. Copyright © 2010 by Pamela J. Hines, Brad Wible, and Melissa McCartney. Published by the American Association for the Advancement of Science. Reprinted by permission of the publisher.

Excerpt from *A Framework for K–12 Science Education: Practices, Crosscutting Concepts, and Core Ideas* by the National Research Council. Copyright © 2012 by the National Academy of Sciences. Published by National Academies Press. Reprinted by permission of the Copyright Clearance Center.

Image credits

Pages 37, 38, 43, 72, 75, 76, 77, 80, 81, 87, 91, 94, 95, 96, 97, 98, 101, 102, and 105: Courtesy of *Seeds of Science/Roots of Reading*. © 2014 The Regents of the University of California.

Pages 46, 47, 83, 84, 89, 100, and 103: Courtesy of *Amplify Science*. © 2018 The Regents of the University of California.

Cataloging-in-Publication Data is on file at the Library of Congress.
ISBN: 978-0-325-11232-9

Series Editors: M. Colleen Cruz and Nell K. Duke *Editor:* Katherine Bryant
Production Editor: Sonja S. Chapman
Typesetter: Drawing Board Studios
Cover and interior designs: Monica Crigler
Manufacturing: Val Cooper

Printed in the United States of America on acid-free paper
23 22 21 20 19   RWP   1 2 3 4 5

CONTENTS

INTRODUCTION

M. Colleen Cruz

The Bronx classroom was abuzz with first graders concentrating on their circuits. Their hands tinkered with wires, battery packs, play dough, and light bulbs. Their conversations centered on strategies—what worked and what didn't. They were surrounded by a classroom library, with books about scientists and circuits displayed within easy reach. The teachers gathered to study together in this classroom asked a quick clarifying question here, gave a quick tip there, but were otherwise not needed as the students, one after another, made their clay creations light up.

Later, these same kids were asked by their teacher to tell the stories of their earlier circuit work. The students grabbed writing paper—the same place where they grabbed paper for their writing workshop stories and books—and got right to work. They crafted stories filled with struggle and triumph, created illustrations that conveyed emotion and that were labeled with discipline-specific vocabulary. The energy in the room could have lit up a small city. One of the teachers observing looked up and said, with tears in his eyes, "This is so amazing. And this is what it could be for every child."

As I stood in the classroom and took it all in, I couldn't help but think of what Jacquey Barber and Gina Cervetti have written in the book you are currently holding. They show us, through both anecdote and research, that what those first graders were doing was not an anomaly, but rather what all teachers of science can be doing. There is simply no reason for science to be taught disconnected from accounts of the work other scientists have done—the scientific literature. In fact, there are countless completely doable and natural ways for teachers to bring science and text instruction together. When we do, our science instruction is both more effective and engaging and also more aligned to what actual scientists do in their field. Scientists don't engage in hands-on experiments without purpose. Scientists don't fill out worksheets to share their findings. And scientists most certainly do not ignore the latest literature on their topic of study.

Throughout this book Jacquey and Gina remind us that scientists do purposeful experiments, share their results with others in meaningful ways, and learn from others' discoveries and that these same things are both authentic and effective ways to teach science as well. In this book, Jacquey and Gina give us not only the lenses to see the instructional possibilities but also the research that undergirds it all.

ACKNOWLEDGMENTS

Many of the ideas and the work shared in this book are the result of years of collaborative work by The Learning Design Group at University of California Berkeley's Lawrence Hall of Science. This dynamic and talented team created the literacy-rich curriculum *Seeds of Science/Roots of Reading* and its successor, *Amplify Science*. We are also grateful to the many teachers and students who have served as partners in this work.

SECTION 1
NOT THIS

All-Text Science or No-Text Science

JACQUELINE BARBER

"Raise your hand if you teach science more than once a week," I asked a group of elementary teachers from a large metropolitan area. Perhaps not surprisingly, few hands went up. The unintended consequences of high-stakes testing had begun to be apparent; the regularly tested subjects of reading and mathematics had become king, occupying the majority of every school day. Subjects like science and social studies were all but disappearing, particularly at the lower grades.

In my work with schools, teachers in multiple districts said they were told by their principals to not worry about teaching science. I heard from science-loving teachers at more than one school that they weren't allowed to teach science—they had to sneak science teaching into their days. According to the report on Strengthening Science Education in California, in 2010, "only 11% of principals surveyed indicated that it was very likely that a student would receive high-quality science instruction in his/her school; an additional 34% said that students were likely to receive such instruction. Twelve percent of principals reported that it was not at all likely that students would receive high-quality instruction" (Dorph et al. 2011, 9). Priorities were clearly elsewhere.

These changed priorities can be seen in the amount of time teachers were able to spend teaching science as compared with English language arts (ELA). According to the National Survey of Science and Mathematics Education (NSSME), the number of minutes teachers reported spending on ELA each week peaked in the year 2000 at an average of 96 minutes per week in grades K–3 contained classrooms and an average of 115 minutes per week in grades 4–6 contained classrooms. The same teachers reported spending an average of 23 and 31 minutes per week on science in grades K–3 and 4–6, respectively (Weiss et al. 2001, 48).

Spending the majority of the day solely on literacy instruction hasn't had the big, positive impact on literacy achievement scores that was hoped for and has not helped science understanding either. In 2018, grades K–3 teachers reported spending an average of 18 minutes per week on science, a 22 percent decrease since 2000. Grades 4–6 teachers reported spending an average of 27 minutes per week, a 13 percent decrease since 2000 (Banilower et al. 2018, 78). Although the pressure to focus on ELA and mathematics clearly took a toll on the amount of science taught in elementary schools, it is not the only reason that so little science is currently taught. Although "not enough time to teach science" ranks highest, other factors such as large class size, lack of professional development, inadequate facilities and lack of resources, low district support for science teaching, as well as teachers' lack of background in science are all cited as reasons by teachers and administrators in over 300 schools in California (Dorph et al. 2011). This study describes the serious erosion of infrastructure needed for science teaching that occurred from 2000 to 2010.

In some places, hands-on science has regained a place in the classroom—but sometimes at the expense of actually learning how to do science, which is the charge of contemporary science standards. The 2018 NSSME Technical Report (Banilower et al.) indicates that 55 percent of elementary teachers have students do hands-on/laboratory activities at least once per week (114), but only 26 percent of teachers reported they have a heavy emphasis on learning how to do science (109). It's as if the goal was to recapture hands-on experiences, rather than to focus on helping students use science practices to build understanding—like scientists do.

In many other places, however, elementary science still is either not taught at all or is presented mainly through text as a collection of disconnected facts. The 2018 NSSME Technical Report indicates that at least once a week, 90 percent of elementary teachers report engaging the whole class in discussions, 85 percent of teachers report explaining science ideas to the whole class, and 37 percent report having students read from a textbook or other material in class, either aloud or to themselves (114). Twenty-seven percent of elementary teachers report having a heavy emphasis on learning science vocabulary and/or facts (109). These activities, although not exclusive to traditional text-dominant approaches to teaching science, are often associated with them. Neither solely text-based nor solely hands-on science is enough. In this book, we'll show you why and how integrating science and literacy instruction supports students' understanding of and engagement with both.

Fitting It All In

Every year the amount of content that teachers need to address grows. On the one hand, teachers feel the pressures of tested subjects and, on the other, a growing list of expectations for what students may experience, depending on the school: health education, school garden, English language development, cooking, engineering design, art, sex education, coding, drug education, music, cursive writing, technology, drama, and so on. Whatever your opinion of the relative importance of these different domains of learning, it is clear that piling on more and more expectations for what students should learn without thoughtful integration and time allocation is a losing strategy. Indeed, teachers who integrate science with other subject areas spend nearly 30 percent more time teaching science than teachers who reported rarely or never integrating science with other subject areas (Dorph et al. 2011, 19).

Fortunately, contemporary standards that have been the result of the movement for fewer, clearer, higher standards (Bill & Melinda Gates Foundation 2010; Rothman 2013) provide help in dealing with this dilemma. These newer standards, and the many sets of state standards that they have inspired, focus on the *practices* of literacy, mathematics, and science: what literate people, mathematicians, and scientists *do*. They also emphasize common elements of what rigorous performance looks like across multiple disciplines. Certain standards in one discipline even sound remarkably as if they would have belonged in another discipline. Consider these:

- Describe a relationship between a series of scientific ideas or concepts, or steps in technical procedures in a text, using language that pertains to time, sequence, and cause/effect.
- Make strategic use of digital media and visual displays of data to express information and enhance understanding of presentations.
- Follow precisely a multistep procedure when carrying out experiments, taking measurements, or performing technical tasks.

It's hard to tell that these are from the Common Core State Standards Initiative (2010) for English Language Arts, not the Next Generation Science Standards! These shared practices can become a strategic place to invest time, helping to resolve the pressures of a bursting-at-the-seams curriculum. This focus does more to support our students as they confront the rapidly changing world, also. The goal of our education system can no longer be to impart a set body of scientific knowledge—we must prepare our young people to exist in a society with an ever-changing base of knowledge and to be ready to solve problems that we don't yet know about.

The three sections of this book show Gina's and my attempt to ease the way forward in an era when keeping each domain only in its own place just can't work anymore.

Goldilocks Was Searching for the Right Thing

Our job as educators often involves breaking complex ideas and problems into smaller pieces and sophisticated practices into component parts. We then create instructional sequences as a pathway to prepare students to take on more complexity over time. In so doing, it can become difficult to keep in mind or even know where to place the emphasis. We lose track of the purpose of our discipline (in the case of science, to understand how the natural world works). We stall out in the intermediary steps, leaving students with a shallow understanding and little experience in engaging with the practices of the discipline. Then we wonder why the experiences we provide our students do not help them use disciplinary practices and core ideas to productive ends. Essential practices (and ideas) can be broken down into component parts, but we do students a disservice if the learning ends there, without helping them move on to the practice or idea as a whole or understand why they have been doing what they have been doing.

Most of us (even those who went on to major in science) learned that science is a body of facts—things that scientists figured out. As students, it was our job to understand these ideas (if we were lucky) or to just memorize them (for the test). Most of us were not taught to see science as a way of thinking and of figuring out how the natural world works—though we might have "known" that in a broad sense. If we did learn this, it was to learn how other people "do science." We didn't typically have the opportunity to begin to think like a scientist or, better yet, investigate the world using the tools of science, until we got to college or even graduate school.

This is not what we want for our students today, and it is not what contemporary standards expect. But many of our teaching practices still lead to this kind of shallow understanding—understandably, because this is how we were all taught.

It is hard to embrace balance if you have chafed when at one extreme or another. Too hot or too cold can drive one to seek out the other extreme, when actually a midpoint between the two extremes would likely have been the right goal. The following section depicts the ineffective extremes of text-dominated science and hands-on-dominated science and what happens when a science program is out of balance.

Text-Dominated Science

Like most of us, I was raised on text-based science and knew the hazards of the read-listen-respond cycle of learning. After reading a portion of the textbook, we would listen to the teacher explain what we had read and then respond to questions. Sometimes that meant responding to questions at the end of the chapter; sometimes it meant responding to the questions on the weekly quizzes or end-of-chapter tests. "Labs" were the only hands-on experiences we had, but they were entirely devoid of "inquiry," serving as verification experiences only, in which students would read or be told "the answer" to a question and then be given the opportunity to replicate that answer in a lab. I don't ever remember student-to-student talk playing a role, except to ensure we were following the step-by-step instructions carefully. I certainly didn't understand why scientists would argue—isn't there a right answer? This was what many of us internalized as the norm.

A more current challenge can be seen in the movement that brought content-area reading in lieu of engaging students in investigations. Content-area reading began with well-intentioned efforts to help students overcome what were viewed as the major literacy-related obstacles to content-area learning: the difficulty of the texts relative to students' reading skills and, particularly, the number of new, difficult words encountered in those texts. The era of content-area reading brought the mantra "every teacher is a teacher of reading" and the expectation that content-area teachers would teach the skills and strategies needed to gain access to school texts in their areas. Providing students with explicit instruction in how to make sense of disciplinary texts has been a wonderful response to reports like the ACT's *Reading Between the Lines* (2006), which demonstrated that inability to comprehend complex disciplinary texts serves as a barrier to learning in the disciplines. However, by focusing so much on reading skills and vocabulary, content-area reading/literacy has often taken too narrow a view of the role of literacy in disciplinary learning.

The literacy strategies offered to teachers through content-area reading often overlooked aspects of reasoning, argumentation, and inquiry that shape literacy practices in the disciplines, instead focusing on low-level skills like memorizing the meaning of words. This also meant that the practices of content-area literacy were often foreign to content-area teachers. Teachers were being asked to teach the skills and strategies of reading about scientific topics in a way that was detached from the work of learning about and doing science (Moje 2008; Moore, Readence, and Rickelman 1983).

Hands-on science activities are frequently viewed as something that can be dropped into a text-dominant curriculum if there's time, where the purpose of the activities is simply engagement. Examples of this include making baking soda and vinegar volcanoes, making cotton ball models of different kinds of clouds, creating an M&M rainbow, or using Oreo cookies to make a model of phases of the moon. While certainly student engagement is a good thing, with regard to science learning, a text-dominant approach, even when studded with fun hands-on activities, clearly relies almost entirely on transmission of information. It is mistakenly considered by many as an efficient way to learn or more crassly as an efficient way to prepare students for large-scale science tests. Involving students in science investigation—the purpose of which is to figure out how the natural world works—is engaging not just because students are doing something with their hands, but because they are using knowledge and reasoning to solve a mystery of nature. And it is what scientists do.

In focusing on reading about science, text-dominated approaches engaged students with a carefully sequenced description of the concepts and facts of science, but they missed the opportunity to help students understand science as a way of figuring out and explaining the natural world.

Many science educators came to view text-dominated science instruction as too distant from the work of professional science and as unlikely to inspire students to pursue careers—or even further study—in science. In many cases, the response was to eschew text and develop approaches to science instruction that would involve students in learning science primarily through activities and investigations. But this approach, too, is incomplete and fails to reflect the work of practicing scientists.

Hands-On-Dominated Science

"What did you do at school today?" I asked my then third grader one day, knowing it was a science day. "It was really fun!" he replied. "We had cups of ginger ale and we put raisins in them, and the raisins went up and down!" Trying to act casually, I responded, "Very cool. What were you learning about?" "Raisins!" he replied, with some exasperation at my apparent thickheadedness. I knew what effort that teacher had gone to, probably buying the ginger ale and raisins herself, spending recess rushing around filling plastic cups with liquid, and then managing twenty-nine eight- and nine-year-olds, spilling, sipping, and tasting the focus of their observations.

Activities like these can provide wonderful opportunities for students to combine their observations and ideas to argue for an explanation of the phenomenon they are observing, but too often they don't. For example, students could have been challenged to figure out why the raisins float then sink then float again? That experience could have been followed by others enabling students to figure out additional properties of liquids and gases. But that didn't happen in my child's class—it was one of a series of stand-alone Friday afternoon science activities, as is the case in too many classes. Perhaps my son's teacher was not clear about the purpose of the hands-on activity herself, or maybe my son was unclear, distracted by the trivial but beautiful phenomenon whereby bubbles of gas attach to the surface of wrinkled raisins sitting at the bottom of a cup of ginger ale, floating to the top of the liquid, and then pop one by one, causing them to sink again.

I, like my son's teacher, too, spent years knocking myself out to provide intriguing experiences to students in classrooms. I was providing them with something to observe and wonder about—an experience that would leave them thinking that science was fun, and they could do it. *I* understood the underlying science, and just the fact that it was there, and I understood it, made this more scientific than, say, mixing paints. I was sure of this even though I knew that students might not understand why, or wouldn't remember if they did, or that students mostly didn't even care why, for instance, the raisins floated and sank. I felt proud because I was engaging them in hands-on science. I was providing students with rich experiences with physical phenomena, about which they might wonder and might some day remember back to and draw upon.

It is common, especially in the early elementary years, to engage students in the *processes* of science, like observing a phenomenon such as the raisins, without connecting those experiences to the larger *purpose* of science. You can see this in what I call "holiday science": putting marshmallow chicks in a microwave, dissolving candy hearts in water, melting and bending candy canes, or making boats out of mini pumpkins. But science isn't about the wow of observing transformations. Science involves asking and answering questions about the natural world. When young students are given the opportunity to observe objects or substances but aren't asking questions or figuring out answers, this isn't doing science. The plant-a-bean activity in which young students plant a lima bean and watch it grow can be an example of this, if watching is all they're doing.

It's not that some of these activities aren't well crafted—they may be grounded in a solid constructivist approach, following an elegant guided discovery cycle of learning: explore, construct, apply. Many, though, are not. Although observation in science is certainly important, I would not categorize the plant-a-bean activity as science. Why is that? Because students are not focused on asking and answering a question or understanding the underlying process.

An extreme focus on hands-on science without incorporating other ways of learning and communicating—reading, writing, talking, and listening—also keeps students from engaging in science as scientists do. Literacy practices that involve making sense of text, engaging in argument from evidence, constructing scientific explanations and arguments, and organizing and communicating ideas are central to what scientists do. Science needs literacy. The converse is true as well—literacy needs science (or another discipline). Literacy is a means to an end—comprehension and communication. When there's nothing to figure out or communicate, engaging in literacy practices serves no purpose. In the rest of this book, we'll look at how thoughtful integration of science and literacy can lead to a real understanding of science, not just "school science," for our students.

How Integrating Science and Literacy Instruction Supports Students in Both Areas

GINA N. CERVETTI

In Section 1, we described how neither hands-on-dominated nor text-dominated science prepares students for the higher-level engagement and learning in both science and literacy. In this section, we will look at what research tells us about the authentic role that literacy plays in science and what we know about integrated science and literacy instruction. Based on this analysis, we'll offer three research-supported principles for effective integration of science and literacy. In the next section, we'll look at the practical steps you can take to translate those principles into effective instruction.

The Authentic Role of Literacy in Science

Until fairly recently, many committed science educators downplayed the idea that reading and writing play an important role in learning science. To some extent, these educators were reacting to a generation of science materials and instruction that had students learn science *solely* by reading textbook chapters and answering questions about the content. In other words, these programs taught science as a set of *facts to be learned or concepts to be mastered.*

Learning science from reading textbooks conflicted with the type of science education being advocated by scientists, many science educators, and the National Science Foundation. These groups had an interest in involving students in *learning science by doing science*—approaches that teach science not as a set of facts but as a way of asking and answering questions about the natural world. Inquiry-oriented approaches that involve students in actual scientific investigations (asking questions, gathering data, and making sense of those data) were seen as a way to support students in understanding how science works and how scientific knowledge is created. Advocates of inquiry-oriented approaches believed that involving students in firsthand investigations more closely reflects the

You may have heard the term *disciplinary literacy*. This term is often used as a counterpoint to *content-area literacy*, which offered teachers general strategies and routines for supporting students in reading and writing content-area texts. Disciplinary literacy (e.g., Moje 2008) approaches literacy as a central part of learning and practice in the disciplines. Several efforts have been made to describe how literacy practices differ across disciplines and how those differences are related to the reasoning and inquiry practices that define each discipline (Goldman et al. 2016). In this book, we are discussing only science literacy, but the approach described falls under the umbrella of disciplinary literacy.

work of practicing scientists and that it is more likely to nurture a love of science. This was broadly considered to be better preparation for science careers—a major concern of the National Science Foundation—and for a lifetime of critical consumption of science information.

In recent years, however, many advocates of inquiry-oriented science have come to recognize that gathering and making sense of data through investigations is only part of the work of doing science. Perhaps more importantly, inquiry-based curriculum programs have started to reflect a broader view of science learning, acknowledging that scientists *also* learn about science from texts, and reading, writing, and communicating orally. All *are* authentic aspects of practicing science. In a special section on literacy in the journal *Science*, Hines, Wible, and McCartney (2010) write:

> Science is about generating and interpreting data. But it is also about communicating facts, ideas, and hypotheses. Scientists write, speak, debate, visualize, listen, and read about their specialities daily. For students unfamiliar with the language or style of science, the deceptively simple act of communication can be a barrier to understanding or becoming involved with science. (447)

The Many Ways That Scientists Use Literacy

- Read to find out what other scientists in the field have learned to design their own research as well as stay abreast of the latest work.
- Write proposals that essentially serve as arguments for why a proposed research initiative should be funded.
- Read and evaluate others' proposals and papers as part of a peer-review process.
- Write to document their data collection.
- Engage in argumentation within a research team to interpret results and plan next steps.

- Write scientific papers that communicate research findings and infer broader meaning.
- Engage in both oral and written discourse to clarify meaning of one's own or another group's research study.

Science educators have started to rethink "text-free" science and have become increasingly interested in the roles of reading and writing in learning and practicing science.

The Role of Literacy in Science Learning

Reading, writing, and talk are authentic parts of scientific practice, and they are also necessary to support students in learning about science and making sense of their scientific investigations. Although participation in science inquiry is a critical part of learning about science, students can't learn everything we want them to know about science through first-hand investigations alone. That is, there are many things that we want students to understand about the natural world that can't easily be observed or manipulated in a hands-on way in classrooms. These include such things as the workings of the human body's internal organs, the movement of objects in the far reaches of our universe, and the composition of matter. Although students can simulate some aspects of these phenomena with models, they need to depend on others' explanations to gain a deeper and more comprehensive understanding.

As one example, students can learn a tremendous amount about magnetic force through hands-on investigations with magnets, but there are many questions that can't be answered through firsthand investigations with magnets, such as what makes magnets attract some metals but not others? Answering this question—and many scientific questions—requires access to outside resources, like texts or scientific experts, and thus depends on students' abilities to access those recourses by reading or communicating about science.

In reality, *most* of our factual and conceptual knowledge is acquired through secondhand explanations from texts and other people. We have learned about historical figures and events, the geology of our planet, the name of every organism, and the workings of governmental systems because we read or heard about these things. Similarly, even professional scientists have gained *most* of their scientific knowledge from secondhand sources.

Reading and Writing Should Not Replace Firsthand Investigations

In asking that we reconsider the roles of reading, writing, and talk in science learning, we are not suggesting that science learning should exclude firsthand investigations. Although students can't learn everything we want them to know about science through direct experience with phenomena, it is also the case that they can't learn everything we want them to know about science through reading and writing alone. Firsthand investigations support depth of understanding by connecting facts and concepts to experiences with real and modeled phenomena. Imagine, for instance, having students investigate magnetic force without ever feeling the pull between two magnets, or merely reading about science and engineering practices without the opportunity to figure something out by using and comparing two different models of a phenomenon. Experiences bring ideas to life.

Moreover, although reading and writing are essential science practices, they do not alone enable students to engage with other practices related to scientific investigation, such as gathering data from observations of phenomena or creating and critiquing models. That is, they do not help students acquire many of the cognitive and practical skills of science. To be scientists or critical consumers of science information, students need to understand not just the "information" or concepts of science but how scientists come to know that information—how they conduct their investigations, what they accept as evidence, how they draw conclusions, and how and why those conclusions are sometimes flawed.

Although most facts and concepts are learned through secondhand sources, including texts, most skills and habits of mind are developed mainly through practice and coaching. Students can only fully learn the skills and practices of science by pursuing questions using the methods of scientific investigations.

A More Balanced View

In a rich and critically important domain like science, we want students to learn both the knowledge and the skills that help them understand how the world works, make good decisions by evaluating scientific information critically, and investigate issues scientifically. Thus, to avoid the trap of textbook-only science or inquiry-only science, we need to aim for synergy—engaging students in using firsthand experiences and text-based experiences as connected parts of investigating questions about the natural world. We need to treat literacy activities and instruction in science not simply as a means to understand or produce texts, but as part of the set of practices in which scientists engage as they ask and answer questions about the natural world. As Ford (2009) points out, we should think about authenticity in science as a shift toward "a more balanced image of practices that involve reasoning and argument, the development of explanations, and the sharing of ideas with colleagues" (387). Scientists aren't scientists if they only read about established knowledge or if they build knowledge only through experiments of their own.

The good news is that this kind of integrated learning not only enhances science learning but also has benefits for students' literacy development. Learning about and practicing science requires sophisticated and specialized skills and knowledge for reading, writing, and talk and provides a rich and engaging context to teach students to engage with informational texts. As we will describe, research offers road maps for using science to support students' informational reading and writing.

Next, we share three principles of science-literacy integration that support this balanced view of the relationship between literacy and scientific investigation and understanding. We describe the research that supports each principle and share examples of instruction that has had positive impacts on students' science learning, reading and writing growth, and motivation.

Principle 1: Frame student investigations with a scientific purpose.
Principle 2: Integrate "hands-on" science with literacy to support science learning.
Principle 3: Help students read, write, and discuss text in science.

Principle 1: Frame Student Investigations with a Scientific Purpose

As we've described, school science is often presented as a set of separate, disconnected experiences, done at the teacher's request or as a set of facts to be learned, presented in texts. There's good reason to think that having more authentic, connected purposes supports student learning in both science and literacy—and that combining science and literacy can help focus instruction on these more meaningful scientific purposes. Teaching with authentic purposes supports students' motivation, their growth in understanding science ideas and scientific inquiry, and their ability to read and produce scientific texts.

There are two key ingredients to teaching with a purpose: the first is that each lesson or activity is linked to a broader goal that represents a real pursuit in the domain (e.g., solving a scientific problem; acquiring an understanding about a natural phenomenon that reveals the world in a new way; reading a text to use, discuss, or write about a scientific question or problem), and the second is that students are aware of the bigger goal they are pursuing.

In science education, the most important purposes are those that are consistent with the goals of professional science: working collaboratively to develop evidence-based explanations about how the natural world works. As Berland et al. (2016) explain:

> Ideally, if a student were asked: "Why are you doing this activity?" they would say, "To help us figure out how and why [a particular phenomenon] happens," rather than, "Because the teacher (or worksheet) asked us." (1086)

Science is a method for understanding the world and solving problems, and the best science instruction engages students in using science for these purposes.

Authentic Purposes Support Motivation and Learning in Science

Numerous studies have found that developing scientific questions and problems that relate to life outside of school brings immediacy and relevance, fostering both motivation and students' understandings about science (e.g., Buck et al. 2014). In a review of research on student interest, motivation, or attitudes in K–12 science, Potvin and Hasni (2014) conclude that science teaching that aims to anchor instruction to real-life problems and experiences has positive impacts on students' interest, motivation, or attitudes. The more than 200 studies the authors reviewed included a wide variety of approaches to creating these anchors, including examining topics that were relevant to students' everyday lives or using case studies of real-world problems to drive students' investigations. For example, students in one study used science investigations to solve a case that involved helping an individual create the right soil conditions to grow a fruit tree. In another study, students engaged in a forensic science unit in which they attempted to solve a crime using science. Some of these purposes were grounded in real problems, and some were based on problem-oriented, but fictional, "cases" (such as the crime scene unit), but all of the studies oriented science instruction around realistic and engaging questions or problems. These examples also differ in the extent to which they address actual problems or needs related to students' communities or experiences in the world. Ideally, on the continuum of fictional to real, real texts and problems are probably more supportive of learning, and on the continuum of distant to close in terms of proximity to students' lives, close is probably better.

Similarly, Kang and Keinonen (2018) used a large international data set to examine factors that influence science interest and achievement. They found that using topics that are relevant to students and society and explaining the relevance of those topics positively influenced students' science learning and achievement.

Investigating Authentic Issues in Students' Lives and Communities

Ideally, students learn science as they use the knowledge and tools of science to examine questions that arise in their lives and communities. This can take shape through community-based investigations. Barton and Tan (2010) offer an example in their study of ten- to fourteen-year-old students engaging in a yearlong investigation of whether their city exhibited the urban heat island effect. The authors trace how the project shifted students' ways of engaging with science and their communities as they participated in systematic study of whether and how the characteristics of landscapes in their community contributed to urban heat island effect. The students engaged in firsthand investigations and reading for additional information; talked about their work with residents, legislators, police officers, and other scientists; and produced high-quality documents and documentaries.

In another example of using science for community problem solving, Belland et al. (2016) describe how middle school students investigated water quality in their local river and made recommendations about ways to improve the water quality. The researchers documented positive outcomes on students' abilities to solve scientific problems and their understanding about the nature of scientific knowledge.

Students can use scientific investigations to learn about many aspects of their lives and communities from water use and quality in their schools and homes to sustainable ecological practices to the native and invasive plants and animals in their communities.

As we will explore in greater depth in subsequent sections, pursuing authentic questions in science necessarily involves both firsthand investigation and reading, writing, and talk.

Authentic Activity Supports Motivation and Learning in Literacy

One reason that integrating science and literacy is beneficial for students is that literacy also becomes more purposeful when it is learned and used in the context of scientific investigations. And, as in science learning, having real reasons to read and write supports students' literacy development and motivation (e.g., McKeown, Beck, and Blake 2009; Purcell-Gates, Duke, and Martineau 2007).

One of the most compelling studies of authenticity in literacy instruction comes from Purcell-Gates, Duke, and Martineau (2007). The researchers documented the extent to which literacy instruction during science time in second- and third-grade classrooms was authentic—that is, relied on the kinds of texts that are used outside of classrooms and used reading and writing for purposes that are used outside of school and for reasons other than learning to read and write. For example, writing a brochure that would be used in a nature preserve was considered an authentic writing activity. The authors found that authentic activity was positively related to students' informational reading comprehension in grade 2 and grade 3 and was associated with students' growth on some dimensions of their informational and procedural writing.

In a recent review of studies of effective literacy teachers, my colleagues and I (Duke, Cervetti, and Wise 2016) found that offering students opportunities to engage in purposeful and applied literacy activities was one of the distinguishing features between more and less effective teachers of literacy around the world. In particular, the most effective literacy teachers linked instruction in discrete literacy skills to reading and writing texts and often provided purposes for writing beyond teacher evaluation.

Science as a Context for Authentic Literacy Instruction

When reading becomes part of how students inquire about the natural world or work to solve a problem, students have a real reason to read. Approaching reading with a compelling purpose can increase students' engagement with the text they read. The same can be said of writing; when students are excited to share their findings or argue for the superiority of their solution, they are more motivated to write in clear and compelling ways.

There is evidence that connecting reading to firsthand experiences in science nurtures students' overall motivation to read, as well as their comprehension skill. Guthrie et al. (2006) provide direct evidence of a link between firsthand experiences and students' growth in reading motivation and comprehension skill. In two third-grade classrooms, students were engaged in a program, *Concept-Oriented Reading Instruction* (*CORI*), that linked reading instruction around nonfiction and fictional texts with firsthand science investigations. In two of the four classrooms, students were involved in a high number of "stimulating" (firsthand) tasks as they read about science topics. Students engaged in observations and experiences such as dissecting owl pellets, taking a habitat walk in a woodland, and making observations of a pond. These activities led to more question-posing, hypothesis formulation, and drawing conclusions from data. In the other two classrooms, students engaged with the same reading materials, strategy instruction, and other supports for reading motivation, but they had many fewer stimulating firsthand experiences. Students who participated in the group with the high number of stimulating tasks made greater growth in reading comprehension. In addition, these students reported higher levels of general reading motivation after the instruction than did students in the classrooms with fewer stimulating tasks. The causal chain established by the researchers is particularly interesting: stimulating tasks led to higher levels of motivation, and higher levels of motivation led to improved reading comprehension. So, using science activities to build students' motivation to read was a powerful support for improving their reading. In another, related study, Guthrie, McRae, and Klauda (2007) found that increasing students' interest in particular texts (situated interest) over time led to increases in overall reading engagement and motivation. When Guthrie, McRae, and Klauda looked across a large set of studies of *CORI* for impacts on motivation, they found moderate impacts on students' enjoyment in learning from text, willingness to try hard to understand difficult text if it was interesting, enjoyment of reading for long periods, and belief in their capacity to read well. *CORI* also had a positive impact on the amount students reported reading for enjoyment.

Principle 2: Integrate "Hands-on" Science with Literacy to Support Science Learning

Integrating inquiry-oriented science instruction with opportunities to read, write, and talk reflects real science practice and supports students' science learning. As described in Section 1, for many people, "doing science" is synonymous with engaging in "hands-on science." And some curriculum programs have been based on the idea that firsthand investigations and discussion are the best way to learn science. However, more authentic approaches to science learning bring together hands-on experiences and text-based experiences in ways that better reflect how scientists learn and practice science and, as such, enable students to experience science in ways that develop stronger understandings of its concepts and practices. In addition, approaches that integrate first-hand investigations with a focus on reading, writing, and talking about science have demonstrated more positive impacts on students' science learning than those that focus on firsthand inquiry alone.

Examples of Purposeful, Integrated Science Literacy Instruction/Performances

- Students use reading and firsthand investigations to pursue questions about the natural world that are closely connected to students' lives and experiences.
- Students use reading and firsthand investigations to pursue questions or solve problems that are relevant to the school and civic community.
- Students pursue deep understandings about the natural world using ongoing investigations.
- Students investigate to produce informational materials for an audience outside of the classroom (e.g., articles or books for another class, brochures for a park or museum, presentations for community members).

The Limits of Kit-Based Programs

Inquiry-oriented approaches to science have often taken the form of kit-based programs, which involve students in a series of firsthand investigations using a wide array of materials. Although firsthand experiences are critical for learning science, not all inquiry-based instruction is equally effective, and research on the kit-based programs has not provided strong evidence of effectiveness (Slavin et al. 2014). Based on a systematic review of twenty-three experimental studies of elementary science programs, Slavin et al. found that kit-based programs did not have overall positive impacts on students' science learning (with an average effect size near zero), but approaches that supported teachers in incorporating cooperative learning, science-literacy integration, and technological tools showed potential for improving students' science learning. The lack of effectiveness of kit-based programs may be because the primary focus on using materials sometimes draws attention away from a focus on building deep understanding about science ideas. As research in the following sections demonstrate, programs that integrate firsthand investigations with reading, writing, and talk have shown more positive impacts on students' science learning.

Science-Literacy Integration That Supports Science Learning: Examples from Research

Augmenting students' inquiry experiences with texts that extend concepts and contextualize their investigations in the natural world provides a way for students to learn many science concepts *and* to experience science as a way of learning about the world. This powerful combination has been shown to improve students' science learning. Several studies have demonstrated the positive effects of integrated science-literacy instruction on students' science learning.

Text *and* Hands-on Experiences Versus Each Alone

In one study, Anderson (1998) examined the impact of interesting texts and hands-on science experiences on, among other things, students' learning of science concepts. Fifth graders participated in one of three instructional interventions—one that combined interesting texts and science observations, one that involved only science observations, and one that involved only interesting texts—or a control group of students that did their regular classroom science instruction. The interesting texts for two of the groups included expository trade books about crabs, turtles, and other animals. The observations for two of the groups involved firsthand observations and interaction with live turtles and hermit crabs. Students in all three of the treatment groups wrote notes, including questions and answers, in a log. Even though all students received the same amount of instruction, the students who read interesting texts and engaged in the science observations gained more conceptual knowledge than students in any of the other groups; that is, they were better able to write an explanation about how crabs and turtles live and grow. Anderson explains that students' firsthand observations of the crabs and turtles generated interest and sparked questions about the animals. Students were motivated to consult texts in order to answer their questions. Their reading of the texts led to more questions, which inspired them to access additional texts, creating a cycle of involvement with interesting and concept-rich texts.

Seeds of Science/Roots of Reading

Providing students with opportunities to learn through multiple modalities—doing, reading, writing, and talking—can be a robust way for students to learn as it allows for repeated opportunities for them to engage a set of core ideas and to apply their emerging understanding as they engage through each modality.

In our work on the *Seeds of Science/Roots of Reading* (University of California, Berkeley 2014) program, we involved students in using firsthand experiences, reading, discussing, and writing (what we have called the "do, talk, read, write" model) to develop understandings about science concepts, the nature of science, and the process of inquiry. For example, if the goal is for students to understand where sand comes from and how it forms, they might observe sand using a variety of tools, discuss their observations, read a book about a scientist who studies the composition of sand, and write their conclusions about the formation of a particular sample of sand.

One of our main principles underlying *Seeds/Roots* instruction is that texts can and should be used in a variety of roles in support of students' inquiries—in ways that are similar to scientists' use of texts. To this end, students read texts that support every aspect of their first-hand investigations and augment their conceptual understandings. For example, students read books that model the inquiry processes that they will use in their own investigations. These are often narratives of a related investigation or biographies of the work of particular scientists. Students also search field guides and handbooks for information that they can leverage as they investigate. For example, students might use a field guide to identify signs of animals as they walk in the woods, or they might use a handbook about how light interacts with various materials to make sense of their own observations of light. As we planned *Seeds/Roots* units on everything from soil to the solar system to chemical reactions, we first identified conceptual end goals and a progression of smaller ideas and understandings that built toward the end goals. Then, using a fairly traditional inquiry cycle as a guide, we identified experiences that could move students along a progression of understanding. These experiences might include involvement in hands-on investigations, reading, writing, or discussions. Examples of this included teaching students how to make and record observations or how to leverage evidence as they wrote explanations.

In an experimental evaluation of a *Seeds of Science/Roots of Reading* unit on light and energy, we found that fourth-grade students made greater growth in their science understanding than students in comparison classrooms that were teaching the same science concepts but doing so using their regular curricula, which included a range of programs from textbooks to kit-based programs (Cervetti et al. 2012). Other research on the approach had demonstrated similarly positive impacts on students' science and literacy learning (Bravo and Cervetti 2014; Cervetti et al. 2007; Wang and Herman 2005).

This research and other studies discussed later demonstrate the power of approaches that bring together questioning, thinking, talking, reading, arguing, and writing in support of students' science learning. Two additional programs, *Science IDEAS* and *CORI*, have also shown positive effects on students' literacy learning, including their passage comprehension, multiple text comprehension, and word recognition. Both programs are discussed with Principle 3.

Principle 3: Help Students Read, Write, and Discuss Text in Science

Over the last two decades, reading educators have become increasingly interested in differences between learning to read fictional narrative texts and learning to read the expository texts that constitute much of school reading beyond the primary grades (Duke and Bennett-Armistead 2003; Palincsar 2005). There is now strong consensus in the reading education community that students need to be taught how to read texts of different genres (RAND Reading Study Group 2002; Common Core State Standards Initiative 2010). School science texts and textbooks have distinct characteristics, such as difficult vocabulary and particular kinds of text features (e.g., diagrams and headings) and structures (e.g., cause-effect and descriptive). It is important to support students' access to science text by teaching these words, features, and structures. In Section 3, Jacquey will describe instruction that supports students' informational literacy skills in the context of science instruction. That is, students need to understand how reading, writing, and talk are different across different disciplinary communities to function successfully in those communities.

Many teachers and educational researchers have come to believe that more closely associating literacy tasks in schools with the kinds of purposes to which literacy outside of school and in disciplinary inquiry has benefits for students' reading and writing development. In addition to supporting positive motivations, purposeful and varied reading and writing helps students to develop more differentiated literacy skills.

Reading, Writing, and Talking Like Scientists

Scientists engage with text differently than professionals in other domains (Shanahan, Shanahan, and Misischia 2011). For example, Yore, Bisanz, and Hand (2003) point to a number of ways that science is different from other ways of knowing, including that scientific explanations and claims must be supported with observable evidence and that scientists must maintain a skeptical stance toward their own and others' evidence. In addition, scientists must report their evidence in ways that leave their claims and explanations open to criticism. These ways of knowing suggest approaches to thinking about literacy instruction in science. For example, reading instruction can emphasize the critical examination of evidence gathered through text and online sources. Writing instruction can help students not only make evidence-supported explanations but also describe their processes and data in ways that allow others to critically examine their work. Students can also engage in the kind of talk that invites them to co-develop their evidence-based explanations and critique each other's evidence (Cervetti, DiPardo, and Staley 2014). The integrated science-literacy programs that have shown positive effects for reading and writing provide clear and explicit instruction in reading and writing informational genres, using the context of science and ongoing question-driven science investigations to support that work.

Evaluating Text Critically

Among the skills needed to be consumers of science information is the ability to critically evaluate the claims being made in science text using the standards of evidence in science (Magnusson and Palincsar 2004), and the ability to synthesize evidence in the interest of formulating explanations. In addition, to read in science, students need to be ready to revise their thinking based on the introduction of new information. Both reading and science rely on cognitive strategies for sensemaking (called comprehension strategies in literacy education). Providing instruction in how to use strategies, such as questioning, predicting, making inferences, setting a purpose, and so on, in the context of both reading and science, prepares students to engage in ongoing investigations.

Connecting Text and Experience

One way to support the development of authentic literacies in science is to position students' reading and writing as direct support for their involvement in scientific investigations. For example, students need to learn to read *across* text and experience, drawing on both to investigate questions about the natural world. Rather than focusing instruction only on comprehension of individual texts for the sake of learning facts or determining the main ideas, reading comprehension in science should move beyond the individual text to focus on the ability to pool diverse information sources. Students need to learn to bring together prior knowledge, firsthand experiences, and information gathered from texts to engage in question-driven investigations and develop conceptual understandings (Guthrie et al. 1999; Holliday, Yore, and Alvermann 1994). Reading across different sources to make better scientific explanations can be supported by comprehension instruction that emphasizes activating and leveraging prior knowledge, making inferences across texts, and revising one's thinking based on the introduction of new information.

Students do not automatically link their reading and their firsthand experiences in science. Craig and Yore (1995) interviewed students in grades 4–8 to find out what they know about science text and science reading. Although the students regarded reading as an active problem-solving process, they saw it as a process of pulling out and remembering information from the text. They did not consider their knowledge, experiences, or science explorations as resources for understanding their reading.

Science-Literacy Integration That Supports Literacy Learning: Examples from Research

Efforts to connect literacy instruction with science have demonstrated substantial benefits for students' literacy development, including their reading comprehension.

CORI

Guthrie and colleagues (e.g., Guthrie and Cox 2001; Guthrie and Wigfield 2000; Guthrie et al. 2004) have a long-standing line of research on the motivational dimensions of reading in content-area instruction. They have shown that coupling reading with opportunities to develop expertise and engage in scientific inquiry helps to motivate engaged reading and helps students acquire and use comprehension strategies. The *CORI* framework includes the following five practices:

1. Using content goals for reading instruction
2. Affording choices and control to students
3. Providing hands-on activities
4. Using interesting texts for instruction
5. Organizing collaboration for learning from text (e.g., Guthrie et al. 2004)

The framework also involves instruction in reading comprehension strategies as students investigate topics in science and social studies through reading and hands-on investigations (e.g., examining owl pellets, observing various habitats, and investigating organisms, such as aquatic insects). Teachers help students draw connections between the texts and their hand-on experiences through discussion and the development of portfolios. The portfolios include notes based on students' firsthand experiences, records of questions, inferences and summaries based on students' reading, illustrations and graphical representations, and even physical models (Swan 2003; Guthrie, McRae, and Klauda 2007). Students use the material gathered in these portfolios to write books related to the themes of the units. Embedding literacy instruction in ongoing investigations, including reading and firsthand experiences, had a powerful influence on students' acquisition of reading comprehension strategies across a series of studies. For example, in the study by Guthrie et al. (2004), *CORI* students made greater growth on a composite assessment of reading strategy use compared with students who received traditional strategy instruction.

Science IDEAS

In the *Science IDEAS* program for elementary students, science instruction is integrated with English language arts instruction. Students learn science concepts through both hands-on science investigations and scientific reading, writing, and discussion (Romance and Vitale 1992, 2001, 2011; Vitale and Romance 2012). The researchers and teachers work together to develop concept maps of key science concepts and then plan a range of hands-on activities and literacy activities to engage students in different aspects of these concepts. For example, in a unit about weather, a teacher might develop a concept map around the concept of water evaporation. The teacher would then develop a series of activities, such as discussion to activate background knowledge, or a demonstration using materials, engaging students in a series of hands-on investigations. The teacher would also develop ways to guide students through the text and connect it to the hands-on research, including developing concept maps and close analysis of multiple texts.

The work with text—closely reading, concept mapping, and writing about the ideas in the text—helps students make sense of the science concepts in the texts they read. It also provides insights into how science texts are organized. In addition, through this effort to form connections among ideas and across experiences with reading and students' involvement in multiple hands-on inquiry experiences, students are engaging in the same kind of intertextual work that scientists do as part of their own investigations. In a series of research studies, this approach has resulted in wide-ranging positive impacts for the students.

The researchers consistently find that first- through fifth-grade students in *IDEAS* classrooms make stronger growth on standardized assessment of reading than students in comparison classrooms that are doing separate science and literacy instruction (Romance and Vitale 1992, 2001; Vitale and Romance 2012). They also make greater gains on assessments of science understanding.

Seeds/Roots

In our own work on *Seeds of Science/Roots of Reading* (as mentioned previously), we found that students who participated in the integrated instruction made greater gains than their peers in science writing. In *Seeds/Roots*, cognitive/comprehension strategy instruction was designed to help students use science text in authentic ways—in the interest of gaining expertise, informing investigations, and finding models for investigations and writing. Students read texts with the disposition of scientists, examining evidence and culling information to fuel their own inquires. They are instructed in issues related to science text genres and science reading and writing strategies as they use literacy to support their involvement in investigating and sensemaking.

In the next section, we'll examine what these principles look like in action and what they mean for classroom instruction.

SECTION 3
BUT THAT

Incorporating Literacy Practices That Are Authentic to Science

JACQUELINE BARBER

In Section 2, Gina laid out the role that literacy authentically plays in science, provided an overview of what research says about the benefits of integrating science and literacy, and introduced three key principles for doing so. In this section, I discuss these three principles for literacy-rich science instruction, providing concrete suggestions for ways to put each of them into practice.

Principle 1: Frame Student Investigations with a Scientific Purpose

As discussed throughout Sections 1 and 2, the purpose of science is to figure out how the natural world works and to communicate those ideas through explanations of phenomena, practices that highlight the convergence of science and literacy. Explanations and solutions are the objectives of science and engineering—they are the "ends."

In the first rainy winter after nearly five years of drought, my oldest son's kindergarten teacher arranged for daily walks in the rain. She requested science funds from the school's parent-teacher organization to purchase a class set of waterproof ponchos and rubber boots. Each day, she had these young children, who were encountering a set of phenomena that were mostly new to them, see what they could figure out. What shape and size are rain drops? Are they always the same shape and size? What does rain do to the playground? Where do the puddles form on the playground? Why? Are there any parts of the playground that we think might flood? Where do the birds go when it rains? And so on. One day, several parents, knowing me as a science educator, asked me how going on walks in the rain was science. I remember my answer: that the difference between a walk in the rain and a science investigation is the purpose that is given to the walks; in science the purpose is to figure out how the natural world works and to use their emerging language to construct explanations of the phenomena they observed. Actually having a scientific purpose—a question to answer, a phenomenon to figure out—is necessary to doing science, as is communicating the resulting explanation or solution.

Scientists Push to Answer How and Why

Let's think back to the example of the floating raisins activity introduced in Section 1. What was the purpose of that activity? It is very common to use an activity like this, or putting Mentos in soda or the creation of slime, as simply an ohh-and-ahh experience. These phenomena are fascinating, and fascination is an important driver of success in science, as are opportunities to explore phenomena. However, stopping at exploration and fasination, without narrowing in on a question to answer, denies students the opportunity to figure something out like a scientist does. Starting out the floating raisins activity discussed in Section 1 by challenging students to figure out why the raisins float, sink, and then float again in the ginger ale provides a clear question and focus to students' scientific investigation. Being able to answer the question, Why do the raisins float?, becomes the scientific purpose. Students still experience the ooh and ahh and can explore, but they also are engaged in figuring out why something happens—which is what scientists do.

Setting Purpose

For each science unit you present, foreground the goal of having students figure something out. Whether students come up with what they want to figure out or whether you provide that focus, the essential element is that students' investigations are driven by a question.

> **Ask yourself: What science phenomenon are students working to figure out?**

Unit Questions

For each unit you present, provide your students with an overall unit question that they will try to answer or a problem they will solve. In the case of the floating raisins phenomenon, the unit question could be: Why do the raisins float, then sink, and then float again in the ginger ale? Or a unit problem could be to design a submarine that can move up and down in the water. You can also have your students come up with a question to answer or a problem to solve, centered on a phenomenon they have observed. Guide students' investigations by referring back to the unit question periodically. Conclude the unit by having the class explain the phenomenon of the floating raisins.

Breaking Down Unit Questions

> **Ask yourself: What is the unit question that will guide students' investigations?**

Let students know that scientists break big questions into smaller questions that are easier to answer. Figuring out the answer to a series of smaller questions can help to answer the big question. The unit question, Why do the raisins float, then sink, and then float again in the ginger ale?, could be broken down into smaller questions: When do the raisins float? When do they sink? Would other objects float and sink and float again in the ginger ale like the raisins do? Would the raisins interact similarly with other liquids? Do the raisins ever stop rising in the ginger ale?

Depending on the age of your students, your instructional goals, and the time you have, smaller questions can be generated by the class, or you can introduce them one by one at opportune moments. Prompt students by asking, for instance, "We have now figured out when the raisins float and when they sink. What additional question can we try to answer that will help us figure out the bigger question of 'Why do the raisins float, then sink, and then float again in ginger ale?' Make these guiding questions visible in the classroom environment and refer to them often. Frequently remind students to think about how answering a smaller question connects to the overall question.

How have I broken that unit question down in to smaller investigation questions?

Focusing on Phenomena, Not Topics

Most of us learned (and helped students learn) about science topics. Science topics are commonly the name of chapters in science textbooks (e.g., amphibians) or the name of science kits (e.g., electricity and magnetism). The current view in the field of science education is that we need to shift from having students *learn about* topics to having students *figure out* science phenomena (National Research Council 2012).

Figure 3.1a and b Students in grade 4 think through the smaller questions to solve weather mysteries.

Name _____ Date _____

Mystery of Weather on the Moon

Does the Moon have weather?

Write your first ideas about this mystery. Do you think the Moon has weather? Why or why not?

I think the Moon has weather because it might be sunny or cold. The weather might be different than here.

Write questions you could ask to help you solve this mystery.

1. Does it rain on the Moon?

2. Is it windy on the Moon?

3. What is the humidity on the Moon?

4.

5.

6.

Name _____ **Date** _____

Mystery of the Drying Towels, Part I

One morning, two wet towels were hung outside to dry. One towel was hung out to dry in Florida and the other was in California. Both towels were equally wet. By the end of the day, one towel was still wet and the other one was dry.

Which towel was dry? Why?

Write your first ideas about this mystery. Why do you think one towel might have dried when the other did not?

Maybe it was hotter in California so the towel dried

faster. Or maybe it rained in Florida.

_____

Write questions you could ask to help you solve this mystery.

1. What was the temperature in Florida and California?

_____

2. Did it rain in Florida or California?

_____

3. What was the humidity in Florida and California?

_____

4. _____

_____

Frame units of study around science phenomena or engineering challenges. Science phenomena are observable events that we can use our science knowledge to explain or predict. They are the things that a scientist notices and investigates. They are the things that make a person curious. All the science instructional materials that were designed specifically to address the NGSS are phenomenon-based or challenge students to solve a problem related to a phenomenon. These and other instructional materials that involve students in figuring things out, including problem-based learning and project-based learning, have in common that they move beyond having students just *learning about* topics.

For instance, rather than setting out to learn about amphibians, we should have students figure out why we don't hear spring peepers at the marshy lot adjacent to the school yard anymore, which leads students to think about the relationship between organisms and environment. Likewise, a unit that invites students to tackle an engineering design challenge, such as to design a way to make fresh water from salt water, provides a scientific purpose requiring that students figure out the phenomenon of water desalinization. Through designing a way to make fresh water from salt water, students will need to find out things about the topic of water, for instance, that liquid water changes to water vapor in a process called evaporation, that salt dissolves in water to create salt water, and that the salt in salt water does not evaporate. Yet these are all things they are learning in service of the need to figure out the phenomenon of desalinization so they can solve a problem. It is through explaining phenomena that over time students construct a broader understanding of a topic.

Your instructional materials may already be structured around figuring out science phenomena and for which an authentic purpose is easy to identify. Or they might need some tweaking. One easy way is to focus on what students will *do* as scien-

If you are wondering whether something is a topic or a phenomenon, ask yourself, "Is it an observable event? Is it something you could figure out?" Topics are not observable events. You can't figure out topics.

Figure 3.2 Differences Between Topic-Based and Phenomenon-Based Units

Topic-Based Unit	Phenomenon-Based Unit
Properties of Materials	How could we make a paint that can be used to cover up graffiti?
Food Webs	What is causing the population boom of invasive mussels in Lake Michigan?
Weather and Climate	Why do there seem to be more and stronger hurricanes than a decade ago?

tists and engineers. Rather than introduce a unit by saying, "In this unit, you will learn about landforms," for instance, frame the unit by saying something like this: "In this unit, you will *act* as geologists to answer the questions, why do landslides happen and where is it likely that landslides may cause road closures." Or, "In this unit you will *figure out how* to make the best glue for use at school."

Connecting Phenomena to Purpose

As you guide students through a unit, make every effort to connect the different activities in which students engage. Ask, "What will this hands-on investigation help us figure out? How is what we have read helpful to the problem we are trying to solve?"

After conducting a hands-on investigation or reading text, focus students on figuring out how the data they collected or information they found can help to answer their question or solve their problem. Have students turn and talk to a partner about their ideas. By connecting students' different experiences to what they are trying to figure out, you can help ensure that there is coherence between what students are doing and what they are thinking.

A network of schools with which I am working uses exit tickets at the end of science time/class that help create a habit of mind among their students to continuously reach to connect what they did with why.

Today's investigation helped us figure out _____.

Today's reading helped us figure out that _____.

The Evolution of "Inquiry-Based" Science

A key difference between the Next Generation Science Standards (NGSS) and previous standards is the use of the term *science and engineering practices* rather than *inquiry*. The National Research Council's Framework for K–12 Education, on which the NGSS are based, points out that *inquiry-based science* has meant different things to different people, whereas the term *science and engineering practices* is able to encompass the broader set of practices in which scientists and engineers engage.

> Our view is that this perspective is an improvement over previous approaches in several ways. First, it minimizes the tendency to reduce scientific practice to a single set of procedures, such as identifying and controlling variables, classifying entities, and identifying sources of error. This tendency overemphasizes experimental investigation at the expense of other practices, such as modeling, critique, and communication. In addition, when such procedures are taught in isolation from science content, they become the aims of instruction in and of themselves rather than a means of developing a deeper understanding of the concepts and purposes of science. (National Research Council 2012, 43)

Following are the broad range of practices in which scientists and engineers engage, which are highlighted in the NGSS.

NGSS Science and Engineering Practices
1. Asking questions and defining problems
2. Developing and using models
3. Planning and carrying out investigations
4. Analyzing and interpreting data
5. Using mathematics and computational thinking
6. Constructing explanations and designing solutions
7. Engaging in argument from evidence
8. Obtaining, evaluating, and communicating information (National Research Council 2012)

I often point out that Practices 1, 2, and 3 are similar to what previous science standards called out (and were synonymous to inquiry for many); Practices 4 and 5 are practices that also appear in mathematics standards; and Practices 6, 7, and 8 resemble practices that appear in English language arts standards. In this way, the NGSS Science and Engineering Practices represent a convergence of practices in science, mathematics, and literacy, all of which are practices used by scientists and engineers use in their work.

Making Science Relevant

There is great value in connecting science learning to actual problems and phenomena that students experience in their classroom or at home. For example, a grade 2 teacher I know noted how her students were always staring out the classroom window at a big beautiful tree where birds often congregated. She modified her unit about habitats to focus on the tree and the birds that spend time there. Teachers in a school in California had their students research, design, and make a plan for their school's garden that included plants that will attract monarch caterpillars. A teacher in Washington, DC, focused his high school students on answering questions about the safety of the school and community environment such as whether their school's drinking water contained lead, what the air quality in subways stations was, and so on. He invited students to inquire about important issues directly affecting them. Think how a unit that is focused on a particular topic (e.g., properties of materials) can be reframed to connect to an everyday phenomenon (e.g., why salad dressing may separate) or to connect to the real problem of creating a way to cool the air in a warm classroom or the problwm of food waste in the cafeteria. Consider opportunities where students can use science and engineering to figure out phenomena and solve problems experienced at school, at home, or in their community.

Figure 3.3 Sample student sheet. Here is another way to prompt student thinking about connections between what they are doing and what they are trying to figure out.

Name _____   Date _____

Making Connections to Your Investigation

1. What is a connection that you can make between your investigation and what you learned about dragonfly nymphs in *Tabletop Pond Guide*?

   _____

   _____

   _____

   _____

2. What is a connection that you can make between your investigation and something you have observed in your group's model pond during the past few weeks?

   _____

   _____

   _____

   _____

3. What is a connection that you can make between your investigation and what you have learned in class about ecosystems?

   _____

   _____

   _____

   _____

4. What is a connection that you can make between your investigation and Hannah and Manny's investigation in *Investigating Crayfish*?

   _____

   _____

   _____

Student Sheet—Aquatic Ecosystems (optional: 2.6)

> Although investigations that feature phenomena such as the floating raisins aren't particularly relevant to students' lives or communities, personal curiosity can make something relevant to a student—I care about it because I am eager to know why that happens! One high school teacher I met demonstrated several different surprising phenomena to students and allowed the students to choose the one they found most interesting to try and explain.

Broadening Students' Worlds and Still Building Relevance

That said, especially as they grow older, students need to be given the opportunity to learn about the broader world, even parts with which they may have little direct contact. For instance, it is not uncommon for me to hear from school districts that because their students don't live near the ocean, that they are not interested in using a unit related to ocean sciences. The fact that nearly three-quarters of Earth's surface is covered by ocean, and that the ocean produces more than half of the oxygen in our atmosphere, establishes the relevance of ocean science to us all—and that's without connecting to all the other ways we depend on the ocean for food, transportation, and more. It's important to enable students to extend their knowledge beyond the current parameters of their lives. Think of connections that can be made to phenomena that happen in places far from your students' communities, such as a unit that is focused on the recovery of a clearcut rainforest in Indonesia (initially cut down to create a plantation for producing palm oil—a common ingredient in food we eat), or another that focuses on how people survive in super dry climates in Africa (with pioneering approaches to water shortages, something increasingly problematic in many parts of our country). Furthermore, focusing on phenomena that are well illustrated in other countries provides culturally relevant connections for students who are recent immigrants from these locales and helps all students become more globally aware citizens.

Planning for Authentic Communication

Part of making science relevant includes giving students authentic opportunities to communicate their results. The following are some specific ways to capitalize on these literacy-rich opportunities.

Ask yourself: How do these phenomena connect to students' lives?

- **Provide an authentic reason for students to share their explanations.** Think of reasons why a scientist or engineer would share their explanations, and see if you can create a parallel situation. For instance, a scientist or engineer might use their newfound knowledge to make a recommendation about the environmental impact of a proposed human-made change, provide an explanation to a community official, create an interpretive brochure or exhibit for visitors, make a prediction about the likelihood of an event occurring, write a letter to the editor, teach someone who doesn't know, create a manual for the user of a product or a safety manual for certain situations, and so on.

- **Provide an audience with which students will share their explanations.** It's ideal when explanations and/or arguments can be communicated to actual audiences, such as other classes at the school, the principal, or the leader of an organization or community organizations, for example. A good second choice can be a fictional or rhetorical audience, such as explaining to the mayor of a fictional city or creating an explanation for a visitor to a national park.

Ask yourself: What could be an authentic reason for students to communicate what they figure out?

Figure 3.4a and b **Sample student sheet.** In this unit, grade 2 students are challenged to design a new and better glue that can be used by the school and to explain their evidence for why it is a good glue.

Name: _____ Date: _____

End-of-Unit Writing: Arguing About a Final Glue Design

Directions:
Complete the sentences in the letter to the principal and in the table below.

Dear Principal _Lopez_____,

As you know, my class has been working to create a better glue for our school. First, we chose the properties we wanted our glue to have and decided on our design goals. These are my design goals:

1. _sticky_____

2. _strong_____

3. _spreadable_____

4. _____

Then, we observed and tested many ingredients. The table below shows the final glue ingredients I have chosen and their properties.

Ingredient	Properties
flour	sticky and strong when mixed with water
cornstarch	makes mixture more spreadable and smooth
water	helps ingredients mix together and be more spreadable

Properties of Materials—Lesson 4.4

Name: _____ Date: _____

End-of-Unit Writing: Arguing About
a Final Glue Design (continued)

I chose these ingredients because together they make a glue that meets my design goals.

_____.

The properties of my final glue are stretchy, but pretty spreadable when wet. When it dries, things stick to paper well even if you try to pull things apart.

I know that my glue meets each design goal because I did a test to see how many washers a glued paper clip would hold, and it held more than 10.

_____

_____.

I hope you will use my glue recipe for our school's new glue!

Sincerely,

Amelia _____

Properties of Materials—Lesson 4.4

Following is a checklist you can use to help ground your science teaching by framing with a scientific purpose and attending to relevance to students' lives and to authenticity of science and engineering.

Principle 1 Checklist: Frame with a Scientific Purpose

☐ What science phenomena are my students going to try to figure out?

☐ What is the unit question that will guide their investigation?

☐ How does the phenomenon connect to their lives?

☐ How have I broken that unit question down in to smaller investigation questions?

☐ What could be an authentic reason for students to communicate what they figure out?

☐ What audience could they share their explanation with?

Principle 2: Integrate "Hands-on" Science with Literacy to Support Science Learning

As Gina described in Section 2, scientists and engineers naturally spend a majority of their time engaged in specialized reading, writing, and discourse for the purpose of investigating questions and solving problems, but school science often deprives students of these opportunities. For example, many times students do a firsthand activity without then engaging in science discourse to make sense of the results, or without consulting a text to help answer new questions, or without communicating findings to an appropriate audience. Each time we fail to include these authentic activities in what students do in the classroom, we miss an opportunity for both meaning and richness, and we create school science experiences that are further and further removed from doing science as professional scientists do.

Following are several suggestions that can help shift a "school science" approach to one that integrates science and literacy thoughtfully and supports students in being able to engage in the kinds of rich performances that science (and contemporary standards) require. These strategies fall in two basic categories: planning for connections and coherence, and supporting students to figure out scientific phenomena by investigating like a scientist does.

Planning for Connections and Coherence

One or two lessons are simply not enough time for students to engage like scientists and engineers. Trying to jam all the thinking, doing, talking, reading, and writing that one needs to do to make meaningful student-centered engagement with scientifically important questions/ phenomena into too little time inevitably results in shortcutting and shortchanging the experience, resulting in little lasting value to students.

A connected and coherent instructional sequence naturally incorporates many literacy-rich moments, often as part of sensemaking. There is no one way to structure a sequence of literacy-rich science activities, but one possibility might look like this.

1. **Students ask questions about phenomena they have observed firsthand or read about.** This will look different according to what students are wondering. You could provide students with phenomena to choose from, such as, Where do the drops of water that form on the outside of a cold drink come from? or Why do regular sodas sink in a bucket of water while diet sodas float? Or you could have students draw questions from things they have wondered. Providing constraint can help students

be successful by ensuring that questions or problems are addressable in the classroom. Whether you curate questions or have students think of their own, anchor the questions with a phenomenon by saying that their question must be a how or why question about something they have observed (or read about) happening.

2. **Students engage in an iterative cycle of gathering evidence from a variety of sources including firsthand investigations and secondary sources and building increasingly complex explanations over time.** Let students know that when scientists work to figure out how and why things happen, they gather evidence from a variety of sources, including firsthand investigations and secondary sources. Ask, "What kind of hands-on investigation could you do that would help answer your question? Where might we look to find information that other scientists have gathered that might help us answer the question?"

3. **Students engage in evidence-based argument to strengthen their explanations.** Provide students with a thinking routine that they can repeat throughout their investigation. One example could be to have students repeatedly reflect on what they are learning by writing and telling a partner: "I found information about _____ by _____. It helps me figure out the answer to my question because _____." Invite partners to ask a series of probing questions: "What makes you think that? How could you be more sure?"

4. **Students write a scientific explanation or argument for a particular audience.** Have students write an explanation for the question they investigated to be part of a book the class publishes. The book could be written for students' families and be titled *Things Room 4 Figured Out*. Because we adults learned the answer to "what" questions when we took science in school, many of us don't know answers to "how" and "why" questions.

Another, more extended possibility, might be:

1. **Students read to stimulate interest and set the context for the unit (narratives or informational texts).** For example, the class might choose to read about inventors. Different students choose different books based on their interests. The teacher helps the class see that inventors (engineers) come up with solutions to problems.

2. **Students engage in firsthand explorations or investigations and write to inform others and/or make sense for themselves.** Students choose a problem they want to solve and engage in exploration of possible materials, processes, or ideas that could be useful in solving their problem. The teacher could constrain their choices, by challenging them, for example, to make an invention that uses magnets to solve a problem. Or a teacher could offer a set of possible inventions that she knows would be realistically actionable for students in the classroom.

3. **Students read to inform their investigations (handbooks, mentor texts, descriptive texts, biographies) and write to record and share their in-progress work.** Students continue to engage in exploratory research by consulting secondary sources relevant to understanding the problem they are trying to solve, practices that might be useful, or information specific to their particular solution.

4. **Students continue firsthand investigations.** Equipped with new information and ideas, students design, iterate, and create first prototypes of their inventions.

5. **Students read to learn about scientists who engage in this work—their dispositions, methods of inquiry, approaches to literacy.** The teacher curates texts or portions of texts that focus on specific challenges that inventors faced and how they addressed those challenges. Students reflect on how inventors work toward the continuous improvement of their solutions and are persistent.

6. **Students engage in oral argumentation to refine their ideas and understanding.** Students may choose to iterate their prototypes before presenting them to classmates. They mount design arguments to say why a particular solution is the best, using data or other evidence they have gathered through testing their inventions.

7. **Students use the information they have gathered to share their investigations in talk and/or writing.** Based on feedback they received, students have one more chance to iterate their prototype designs.

8. **Students engage in a challenge that provides an opportunity to apply their knowledge and skills.** They might write advertisements for inventions and demonstrate how they work at an inventor fair for the school.

> **Good science instruction involves a sequence of activities, not single activities.**

Whatever specific sequence you use, the bottom line is that students need opportunity and time (just as scientists do) to figure out and cognitively process new ideas. Providing sense-making opportunities that involve students in talking and writing is a great way to do that.

Multiple Modalities: Do, Talk, Read, and Write

An easy way to break out of narrow approaches to science teaching and learning (hands-on-dominant or text-dominant approaches) is to set yourself a goal of providing students with opportunities to engage with each important phenomenon or idea in all four modalities—do, talk, read, write. For instance, a common experience students have is investigating what magnets attract. Students are given a variety of objects made of different materials. The experience typically ends with a debrief in which students conclude that magnets attract metal. Either it is glossed over that there are some metal objects that aren't attracted by magnets, like the ball of aluminum foil, a penny, or stainless-steel pan, or the teacher might explain that magnets attract only some kinds of metal. Instead consider doing the following:

Do: Students predict what objects are attracted to a magnet and test their predictions.

Talk: The class analyzes the data that was collected. The teacher helps draw out a pattern, that magnets seem to attract some metal objects but not all metal objects. They wonder: What is different about the metal objects that magnets attract?

Read: Motivated by this question, students inquire through text to search for evidence about the metal composition of the objects they tested.

Write: Based on evidence they collected from both a firsthand source (experience) and a secondhand source (text), students discuss claims about what sticks to magnets and write explanations incorporating their claims.

Supporting Students to Figure Out Like a Scientist Does

To move closer to the kind of science that professional scientists practice, think about how scientists figure things out. They collect evidence from many sources, including firsthand investigations, physical models, digital models, primary sources (e.g., photographs, audio recordings, video), data other scientists have collected, and trusted secondary texts. Here we'll share some strategies to use as you support your students in investigating scientific phenomena like scientists.

Ask yourself: What will my students be doing in a hands-on way to try to figure out the phenomenon? How will they be reading like a scientist reads? How will they be writing like a scientist writes? When will they have opportunities to engage in talk with their peers?

Activating and Connecting to Prior Knowledge

Scientists begin new investigations by finding all that the scientific community already knows about a phenomenon. Following are some suggestions for how to do this:

1. When possible, provide an initial opportunity for students to explore the phenomenon they will be investigating. This enables more students to have knowledge to activate and contribute to initial discussions.

This exploration could be as simple as providing time for students to browse through an illustrated informational book, watch a video that shares images and information about the phenomenon in nature, or interact in a firsthand way with materials. This step provides students that have less background knowledge relevant to the phenomenon with the opportunity to build some.

Open-ended exploration, in which students explore without a goal, is an essential part of science. This is often a phase when students generate questions, build background knowledge, and frame initial ideas. Exploration typically comes before an investigation question has been decided upon. It's important to be clear about when the goal is to become familiar with substances or phenomena by exploring versus when the goal is to answer a specific question, for instance, about how or why something happens. You might say, "This is a time when we are just exploring, to get to know about X and start to notice what happens when Y. Our only goal is to explore and wonder. When we explore, we may start to have ideas about what causes an effect, and we might start to figure things out. But our goal is to explore and see what we find."

2. Provide access to secondary sources and experts to help students understand procedures and practices they will need to design and pursue investigations—another kind of background knowledge. These might include techniques such as observing a defined study site over time, analyzing animals' scat or owl pellets to see what an animal ate, counting the number of a certain organism in a defined area at systematic intervals, and so on.

Knowing more about these different practices can prepare students to design better ways to set up their investigation of squirrels in the neighborhood or their investigation of the factors that are important for a snail's habitat.

3. Early in each new unit, ask the students what they know about the phenomenon they will be investigating. Record this on a chart that you can revisit later. Title the chart "What We Think We Know About X," and let the students know that this chart represents their beginning ideas. As they learn more, they might find that some of the things they think they know might not turn out to be correct, or maybe they are only partially correct, and that you will revisit this list later. Later in the unit, return to the list of students' beginning ideas. Ask, "Given the new evidence we have gathered, are there any ideas that we think are no longer correct or only partly correct?" Go through the list item by item. Discuss whether students think ideas should be changed. If you notice that there are still misconceptions on the list after this discussion, return to them again later in the unit, after students have had more opportunity to gather evidence and construct deeper understanding.

4. Engage students' prior knowledge by having them make predictions at the beginning of an investigation. Making a prediction is a way for students to cognitively engage with an investigation. It's not important for the prediction to be right; instead, the goal is to orient students to the purpose of the investigation and help them focus their observations.

For example, you could ask students to predict what they think will happen when two substances are mixed. They might say that the mixture will bubble, get hot, or change color. This will sharpen students' focus as they look for evidence of a particular outcome.

If you want to narrow your students' predictions to head off fanciful predictions, or to guide their focus, you might have them agree or disagree with a claim they have read or encountered. Their agreement or disagreement is a form of prediction. For example, you might ask

**Ask yourself:
How will I give
students an
opportunity
to access and
connect to prior
knowledge?**

students to agree or disagree with the claim that "All plants have roots." As they read through an informational text on plants, this will focus students on looking for information about roots and to be on the alert for plants that may not have roots.

Figure 3.5   Sample class chart: "What We Think We Know About Magnets." Students in this grade 3 class corrected their initial idea that magnets attract metal. They did this after they discovered through a firsthand investigation that there are some metals that are not attracted to magnets, and after they learned in a reference book that to be attracted to magnets, metals must contain a certain amount of iron.

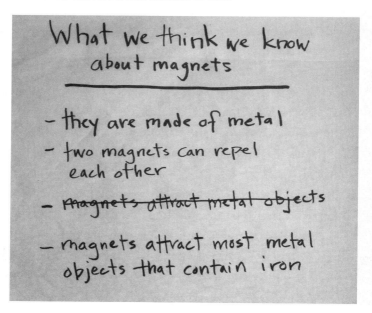

Using Different Kinds of Evidence and Information

Scientists don't just rely on evidence from hands-on investigations, nor do they just rely on evidence from text. Here are some ways to add richness and variety to students' investigations, as well as provide practice in having students consider evidence from multiple sources as they create their explanations.

Let students know that the data that come from hands-on experiences is one important source of evidence they will use to try to answer their question. But there are other sources of evidence, too, such as information from reference books, other scientists' investigations, and primary sources such as videos, photographs, and so on. These primary sources are discussed in more detail later in this section. So, for example, in figuring out the phenomenon of the floating raisins, ask, "Can you think of a way that a slow motion video of the phenomenon could help us figure out how the phenomenon works? What evidence would this allow us to collect?"

It's ideal when you can find a book, article, or video that provides key information that is not observable in a firsthand way, or difficult to obtain in a classroom, and could help students figure out an answer to their question. Other times you might need to curate information to make it accessible for your students. In the floating raisins example, you could create a data table of the weights (or for older students, the densities) of a raisin, a grape, a blueberry, a peppercorn, and any other objects that your students might have tested to see if they would float and then sink in the ginger ale.

Figure 3.6   Sources of Evidence

Firsthand Sources	Secondhand Sources
Investigations with real phenomena Investigations with modeled phenomena Investigations with primary sources	Searching for ideas in texts about science Using data from other scientists

Here are a few specific ways to introduce students to evidence from different types of primary sources:

- **Locate webcams and videos.** There is an amazing array of web-cams on the Internet that can enable your students to observe organisms in their habitats. Students can use these webcams to observe animal behaviors and to ask and answer questions. Videos can also be used to capture the behavior of animals, and they require less waiting around for the subject of study to show up. Most webcams post segments of video that can be viewed and analyzed.

- **Provide photographs, micrographs, and/or x-ray images.** Photos of space objects are available for free through NASA websites. There are micrographs of many organisms that are too small to see. You can find x-ray images of animals online, enabling students to investigate and compare skeletal structures between different animals, and so on. There are endless sources.

- **Show time-lapse and slow-motion videos.** These videos offer ways to "see" things that are too slow or too fast to see directly. For instance, there are time-lapse videos showing phototropism—how plants move toward light. You can find slow-motion videos of a wide variety of insects flying that students can observe, describe, and compare to figure out the mechanics of flight in different organisms. These modified forms of primary source video are used by scientists and engineers as well, as they work to figure out how and why phenomena work.

- **Access scientific data sets.** Check NOAA websites to find weather data from the atmosphere and temperature data from the ocean. Some sites provide real-time data collected as part of scientific studies, for example, on animal migration, for which the location of radio-tagged organisms is tracked. Internet searches can produce data from a huge variety of studies, on just about any topic you want. An increasing number of these sites have student interfaces, though it can be challenging to find sources of data that are both relevant to students' investigations and simple enough for them to analyze. Consider curating a data set and providing it to your students. Pulling out a subset of data into a table can both provide a model of how to organize data and practice analyzing data. For instance, students investigating the patterns of day and night in polar environments would benefit from analyzing data about times of sunset and sunrise over the course of a year.

> **Ask yourself: What is the range of evidence sources students will be accessing?**

Learning to Analyze Data and Interpret Results

Students need support in learning to analyze data and make and support claims based on them. They need to learn to read and interpret data tables, graphs, and other visual representations.

You might model and explain how to read tables and then guide students through a data table, asking questions like "What do you think the words at the top of the column mean? The information is also organized from side to side in rows. What does this number represent? Why is it in this row? Why is it in this column? How many columns do we have in our data table? Why? How many rows are there? Why?" Then ask questions to help them see patterns or relationships in the data, for example: "What is the same about all the numbers in the first column? The second column? Do you see any patterns in the data? For example, are there bigger numbers in one part of the table? Why do you think that might be?" You can use similar questions to help students understand other visual representations and look for patterns and relationships.

It's one thing to analyze the results of an investigation; it's another to interpret what those results mean and connect the results back to the investigation question. It's important to return to seemingly simple questions such as "What are we trying to figure out?" You can't ask this

Figure 3.7 **Class substance table.** A grade 2 class collected evidence about the properties of substances that could be used to make glue.

Class Substance Table

Substance	Properties			
	strength	dries quickly	spreadable	Notes
egg whites		NO ✓✓ YES ✓✓✓	Yes ✓✓	dries quickly too thin
flour	✓✓✓✓✓	YES ✓ NO ✓	NO ✓✓✓	crumbly
corn syrup	✓✓	NO ✓✓✓✓✓	Yes ✓✓	dried really slowly
gelatin	✓✓✓	Yes ✓	No ✓✓✓	thin, runny

Figure 3.8 **Evidence of glue properties.** A grade 2 class collects and synthesizes evidence of good glue properties, from both text and hands-on investigations.

Evidence of Good Glue Properties

Ingredient	Evidence from Handbook	Evidence from Strength Test
egg whites	p.17 can stick things together p.17 used as a glue	0, 0, 3, 6, 0
flour	p.19 sticky when mixed with water p.18 hard when dry	11, 12, 9, 10, 13
corn syrup	p.15 can make a mixture sticky when dry	7, 9, 6 3, 5
gelatin	p.21 can hold ingredients together	11, 8, 11 7, 13

question too often. Asking this question serves to remind students of the focus as they move forward. Tell the class that an explanation is the answer to a question. They are trying to come up with an explanation to answer their investigation question.

Invite students to turn and talk and discuss whether they think they have answered the investigation question (figured out how or why something happens), and if so, what they think the answer (explanation) is. This first foray into creating a scientific explanation is just making sure that students understand the explanation. At this stage, don't worry about how students are articulating their answers (explanations)—the point is for them to have a sense that they understand the "how" or "why."

Engaging with Text as Scientists Do

As Gina discussed in Section 2, scientists engage with text in many ways for many purposes. Here are some ways to bring these same authentic purposes into your classroom.

- Find books or articles that can communicate the relevance of a question or investigation. Text can help students connect their classroom investigation to the world outside the classroom. For example, in the *Seeds/Roots* program, students read a book called *Why Aren't Rain Boots Made of Paper?* by Kevin Beals and P. David Pearson (2007) to learn why understanding about the properties of materials is important, and, in another unit, they read a book called *The Black Tide* by Nicole Parizeau (2007) about an oil spill that happened in Spain before they embark on trying to devise methods for cleaning up an oil spill. Emma Strack and Guillaume Plantevin's (2018) *What's the Difference?* contrasts pairs of seemingly similar animals, weather phenomena, plants, and so on. It sets the context for an investigation that will require careful observation and focus on distinguishing differences. Choose books or articles for your students to read that can engage students, set context, and connect their classroom investigation to the real world.

- Use books that describe the practices involved in a scientific investigation or a design challenge to help students as they devise their own investigations and experiments. For example, the series of books, One Small Square by Donald Silver and Patricia Wynne (1997), that focus on *one small square* in a variety of environments, from the woods, to a pond, a swamp, and a desert, show the variety of plants and animals observable in focused study sites in different environments and provide models of and explicit instruction in various scientific practices that students can then use as they make their own observations of a study site in their yard, at a park, or on the school yard. Students might also read a book called *Jess Makes Hair Gel* (Barber 2007) prior to designing their own glue. These books don't eclipse discovery (although sometimes that's appropriate—when something can't be practically discovered by children on their own); they prepare students to better engage in science and engineering practices.

- Search for resources that provide students with information they can use to support their investigations. For instance, field guides are excellent sources for students to look up information about organisms they are investigating. There is a series of books called Take-Along Guides that are children's versions of field guides including titles like *Trees, Leaves, and Bark* by Diane Burns (1995) and *Tracks, Scats, and Signs* by Leslie Dendy (1995). There are handbooks that contain information about other topics, such as The Smithsonian Handbooks (1992) published by Dorling Kindersley; and trusted internet sites such as those of NASA and NOAA can provide information students need in their investigations.

Putting It All Together

Following is an example of planning a rich and coherent unit of study based on all the ideas we've discussed so far. We'll describe a unit investigating the animals around a school as an example. (This unit can be used in a variety of environments.)

1. Choose a phenomenon for students to figure out that has relevance to them or the real world. Good choices are phenomena that are rich enough to be able to sustain investigation across the length of a unit.

Example: Animals live on our school grounds even though we can't always see them.

2. Create guiding questions to support students' investigation of the phenomenon. Determine a coherent sequence of investigation by ordering unit questions.

Examples:

Unit question: What kinds of animals (including mammals, birds, insects, etc.) live on or near our school grounds?

Subquestions:

A. What animals are easily visible to us, and what evidence can we observe of those animals?

B. What evidence can we observe of less visible animals?

C. Why are some animals hard to see?

D. Why can these animals live where they do?

E. What might make it so these animals can't live there?

3. Decide how you would like your students to share what they have learned and with whom.

Example: Invite the class to create an annotated map of the school grounds, pointing out what organisms were observed and where. The class can create a field guide to the animals found on or around school grounds, including drawings or photos of organisms and descriptions of the habitat needs of each. Having an authentic purpose and audience with which to share their finding, such as to teach school neighbors about the animals in their neighborhood, will only enhance students' motivation and engagement with the investigation process, as well as improve the literacy in their work.

4. Inventory for yourself the possible opportunities students could have to gather information and evidence to figure out the phenomenon and that mirror how science is practiced in the world outside the classroom.

Examples:

- Consider your school environment and the kinds of evidence of animals that students would be likely to encounter. It's possible to find evidence of animals even in urban school yards, including small organisms that may not be easily visible (a great opportunity to encourage students to look beyond the animals they are familiar with).
- Consider the range of realistic options that you may be able to provide your students: basic tools (cameras, clipboards, pencils for sketching, hand lenses); specialized tools that work to help observe hard-to-see animals (e.g., water spray bottles to make spider webs on bushes more visible, "shake-boxes" that enable one to find small organisms in leaf litter, or under bushes; sweep nets); tools to use in characterizing physical differences between different parts of the school grounds (e.g., thermometers, humidity paper).
- Consider a range of techniques that ecologists use, such as: setting up study sites and engaging in close observation over time; counting and mapping the population of animals; and so on.
- Locate possible field experts who could talk to your students and provide additional information and ideas for data collection.

5. Inventory the possible types of rich evidence sources that will support students as they seek answers to the guiding questions, including such things as investigations with real phenomena and/or physical models, primary sources, trusted science texts, data from other scientists, or visits from experts.

Consider the range of evidence sources that might exist.

- Real phenomena: actual observations of the school site, modeled phenomena: such as digital simulations, board games, or physical simulations that can introduce ideas relevant to the phenomenon such as animal defenses, habitat relationships, competition for resources, and camouflage.

- Trusted science sources: field guides of local animals and evidence these organisms may leave (tracks, scat, evidence of having eaten); text-based information about study methods, habitat requirements, defensive structures, and behaviors of specific animals; webcams showing animals in their habitats; videos with relevant information.

6. After generating ideas for ways of gathering information and evidence, and for a variety of evidence sources, take stock of your options. Then build your sequence of student experiences, determining for each question the kinds of data students will need to gather and what authentic processes for evidence gathering and sensemaking students can use. Ensure that your plan has multiple opportunities for your students to do, talk, read, and write including the kind of sensemaking that happens through student-to-student talk and reflective writing to enable them to construct a deep explanation for the phenomenon.

Example, using the questions listed under 2:

    A. What animals are easily visible to us, and what evidence can we observe of those animals?

Have the class consider how one might gather evidence of animals living on school grounds. How do scientists do that? After discussing how one could increase the likelihood of spotting animals, have the class make a plan for observation. Provide students with cameras, clipboards, and paper and pencil for sketching, and have them record what they observe. Have students read about evidence animals may leave (tracks, scat, nibbled leaves, and so on) and go out again looking for additional evidence.

B. What evidence can we observe of less visible animals? Introduce students to one or more techniques that ecologists use to observe animals. Provide students with the opportunity to use these techniques, then to record and share what they observe.

C. Why are some animals hard to see? Provide opportunities for students to learn and think about structures and behaviors that enable animals to be unseen, from text, videos, the Internet, and expert guests. Have students apply what they've learned to explain the situation of animals on your school grounds.

D. Why can these animals live there? Provide opportunities for students to learn and think about the survival needs of some of the animals they are investigating. Small groups of students can take on specific organisms and report back to others, becoming the class "experts" on their organism.

E. What might make it so these animals can't live there? Invite students to predict what changes in the environment (getting hotter or colder) or in available resources (water, food) could threaten the habitat of the animal(s) they observed. What might happen to those organisms if those changes occur?

It turns out that a great guide for a literacy-rich approach to science is to look to the authentic ways that scientists do their work. Scientists and engineers gather information about the world through firsthand experiences and closely related reading of other scientists' findings. Throughout their investigations, scientists engage in sensemaking and communication through talk and writing. Affording students these same opportunities only makes sense. Following is a checklist you can use to help guide your planning.

Principle 2 Checklist: Integrate "Hands-on" Science with Literacy to Support Science Learning

- ☐ What will my students be *doing* in a hands-on way to try to figure out the phenomenon?
- ☐ How will they be reading like a scientist reads?
- ☐ How will they be writing like a scientist writes?
- ☐ When will they have opportunities to engage in talk with their peers?
- ☐ How will I give them opportunities to access and connect to prior knowledge?
- ☐ What is the range of evidence sources students will be accessing?

Principle 3: Help Students Read, Write, and Discuss Text in Science

As Gina explained in Section 2, gaining facility with science text (both print and oral) involves receiving explicit instruction and practice in the many strategies one can use in tackling complex disciplinary text. These include utilizing text features (e.g., diagrams and headings), becoming familiar with the types of text structures commonly used in texts about science, and employing general strategies for making sense of text, as well as synthesizing information from multiple sources.

Similarly, students need explicit instruction and practice in *producing* science language and text. These include helping students make sense of scientific phenomena through written and oral explanation and supporting students to evaluate and critique through evidence-based argument.

Embedding instructional experiences within science investigations allows students to immediately use these practices in the service of science. Following are some ideas for how to do this effectively.

Learning to Navigate Informational Text

Students need to understand how to comfortably navigate informational texts. Informational texts employ a range of structures, text features, and visual representations that are different from those used in fictional narratives. In order to help students learn to navigate informational text, collect a number of different informational books and invite students to look through them. These could include handbooks, field guides, atlases, encyclopedias, directories, or dictionaries. Engage students in conversation about the books. What is similar in the different books? What is different? Explain that unlike fiction, informational books aren't meant to be read from beginning to end; rather, they contain information that a person can look up if there is something they want to find out.

Headings

One key element of understanding informational text is using and understanding headings. Here are some ways to help students learn to navigate through text effectively.

- The first time that students refer to an informational text in their investigation, have them go through the text, reading just the headings. Ask, "What do the headings tell us about the information in this book/article/chapter? What questions do you have after reading through the headings?" Invite students to mention unfamiliar words they encounter in the headings and make note of them. This activity can fuel the creation of a "what we know, what we wonder" list.
- Find a moment in a science investigation when students need to gather information or search for evidence. Choose a section

from a relevant informational book that has helpful headings. Duplicate two copies of the section. Project it first with headings removed. Either read it aloud or have students read it, and then have them discuss what they think the section is about. Now show the same passage with headings. Ask, "How do the headings make it easier to understand?"

- When students are about to read a science text as part of their investigation, provide them with a section of that text without headings. Depending on the age of your students, you might want to duplicate the text, leaving spaces where helpful headings could be, and then lead the class in thinking through what good headings might be. Alternatively, you could duplicate a section for each pair of students, and cut apart all the paragraphs in that section. Have student pairs read, categorize, and then sequence the paragraphs. They can glue them to a sheet of paper, and create headings they think would make the text easy to navigate and understand. Have pairs trade and read each other's headings. Ask, "How are their headings similar? How are they different?"

- Provide pairs of students with a copy of the same informational text. Model using the headings to find a specific bit of information. Then challenge pairs to use the headings to help them answer a specific question they are investigating or wondering about as part of their investigation.

- Invite students to write advice to students in a younger grade about headings or to demonstrate how to use headings to a younger science buddy. How can they use the headings to find what they are looking for or to help make sense of what they read?

Table of Contents and Index

Knowing how to find what you are looking for in a book, short of randomly leafing through, is an important skill and is essential in using informational books. The following are suggestions for ways to engage students in exploring the use of a table of contents and an index as students look for information to support their investigation:

- When students need to gather information as part of their investigations, select a relevant informational book. Think aloud as you model looking for something specific. For example, you could say: "I am looking for information in this book about plant and animal defenses, and I want to read about a hedgehog's defenses. Here I am at the table of contents, and I see that there are four categories of plant and animal defenses: camouflage, shells and armor, spikes and spines, and poison and venom. Where do you think I should look to find information about a hedgehog? Hmm . . . if I'm not sure which category to find the hedgehog, what else could I do? Right. I could turn to the section of the book that I think might be best—I'm going to guess that its spikes and spines—and see if I see the hedgehog listed there. What else could I do? Yes, I could see if there's an index and look to see if it lists hedgehog." Model one or two more times, asking students for guidance as you go. Then provide a topic for all students to find. Ask students to think what specific categories of information might help them with their investigation, and invite them to search in the table of contents to see if they can find a section that will be helpful. Allowing students to choose their own topics as well as choosing what books to look in will lead to more ownership and is more authentic to their role as investigators, but it more often results in students not finding the information they are looking for, so will require more support.
- Repeat how a table of contents is a good and quick way to get to the part of the book that has a category of information relevant to one's investigation. Tell students that an index can be used for the same purpose but can also be used to find more specific information. Think aloud as you share what information you are searching for, and describe each step you take. Again, model this a time or two more, asking students to prompt you by answer-

ing questions like, "OK, now I'm at the back of the book and I see the index. Now what do I do?" Have students think of a question they have and challenge them to use the index to find out more.

Provide students with a list of information that might be useful to them in their investigation. Have student pairs decide whether it would be easier to find the information with a table of contents or an index. Why?

Ask yourself: What aspects of finding information are challenging for my students? What instruction am I providing?

Reading Across Text and Visuals

Some students read text without stopping to look at the diagrams. Others may just look at the visual representations and skip most of the text. Scientists make sense of text by both reading text and carefully looking at the visual representations. The activities that follow can help students begin to read across text and visual representations:

- Choose a section of informational text that has at least one visual representation. Have students work in pairs to first read the text and then "read" the visual representation. Ask, "What does the text say that the visual representation does not? What does the visual representation say that the text does not? What new thing do you understand by thinking about the text and the visual representation together?"
- Have each pair of students trade off playing the role of "text reader" or "visual representation reader." After both have had time to read and make sense of their part of the page, have students talk together to figure out what new understanding they have after thinking about how the words and the picture go together. Before beginning, model doing this with a student as your partner.

Figure 3.9 Student sheet. Students can use this page to keep track of features of information text that they encounter in the book they are reading.

Name _____   Date _____

Text Features Chart

Write the name of the book in the first column. Look through the book to find the different text features. Write at least one page number in the columns to show where you found that feature in the book.

Title	Book Description	Table of Contents	Index	Glossary	Headings/Subheadings	Bulleted Lists	About the Author	Bold Print	Italic Print	Diagrams	Photographs/Illustrations	Captions	Tables

Text Structures

Scientific texts use a variety of structures to communicate information, including thematic clustering, comparison/contrast, cause/effect, problem/solution, and chronological sequences. As you engage with science texts, use strategies that heighten students' awareness of these structures and how they help to communicate science information.

- As you engage in interactive reading, talk about what you notice about the organization of information and the cues in the text that reveal the organization. For example, you might model noticing that a text is describing a problem and predict that some solutions are forthcoming. ("I am noticing that the author is telling us about threats to the ocean ecosystem. I think the author will also tell us about ways that scientists are helping or maybe even ways that we can help. When authors organize texts in this way, we call it problem/solution . . .") Or, you might notice a comparison/contrast text structure and work with students to investigate the presence of cue words. ("The author is comparing frogs and toads in this book. In a comparison/contrast text like this, the author will usually tell us many ways that two or more things are alike or different. As we read, let's try to find words such as *like, unlike, similarly,* and *instead.* These words can tell us that things are being compared.")

- Use text discussions to highlight text structures. Pose discussions that point to the organization of the text. ("We know that this author's goal was to tell us how this scientist figured out how he developed jelly beans of different flavors. What did he do first?") You can also map these text structures using various concept maps and graphic organizers. These can include T-charts or Venn diagrams for comparison text structures and arrow charts for sequences and cause/effect text structures.

- Create opportunities for students to write using a new text structure—in science or throughout the day. Students might compare the adaptations of two organisms as they investigate pill bug and sow bug defenses, or they might propose a solution to a problem in the classroom or school, such as a flooded corner of the playground.

Ask yourself: What explicit instruction am I providing in making sense of complex text?

Figure 3.10a, b, c, and d   Sample graphic organizer. Here is a collection of graphic organizers that students can use to focus on the structure of a text.

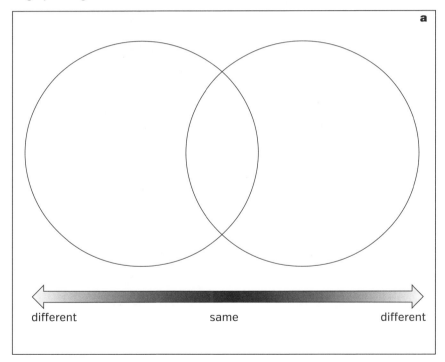

Name _____ **Date** _____

Cause–Effect Text Structure

Title of book: _____

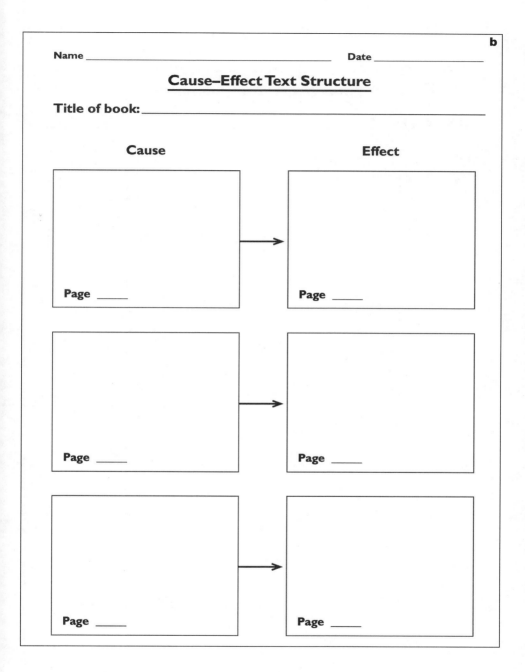

Cause	Effect

Page _____

Page _____

Page _____

Page _____

Page _____

Page _____

Name _____   **Date** _____

Time–Order Text Structure

Title of Book: _____

```
┌──────────────────────────────────┐
│                                  │
│                                  │
│                                  │
└──────────────────────────────────┘
                 │
                 ▼
┌──────────────────────────────────┐
│                                  │
│                                  │
│                                  │
└──────────────────────────────────┘
                 │
                 ▼
┌──────────────────────────────────┐
│                                  │
│                                  │
│                                  │
└──────────────────────────────────┘
                 │
                 ▼
┌──────────────────────────────────┐
│                                  │
│                                  │
│                                  │
└──────────────────────────────────┘
                 │
                 ▼
┌──────────────────────────────────┐
│                                  │
│                                  │
│                                  │
└──────────────────────────────────┘
```

Name _____ **Date** _____

Question–Answer Text Structure

Title of Book: _____

Question	Answer

Comprehending and Synthesizing Information from Multiple Sources

Rather than focusing instruction only on comprehension of individual texts for the sake of learning facts or determining the main ideas, reading comprehension in science should move beyond the individual text to focus on the ability to pool diverse information sources—prior knowledge, firsthand experiences, and texts—to engage in question-driven investigations and develop conceptual understandings (Guthrie et al. 1999). The next several suggestions provide ideas for how to focus students on using text as one source of evidence, along with evidence from other sources.

- Choose a comprehension strategy that can work well to help students make sense of both text and firsthand investigation, such as setting a purpose. (See Figure 3.11 for more strategies that work well for this.) Before reading a text, work with the class to set a purpose for reading. Model by reading a few pages aloud and then ask, "What is our purpose for reading? Have we met our purpose yet? How will we know when we have met our purpose?" Do the same before students embark on a firsthand investigation. "What should our purpose be for investigating?" Write the purpose on the board. As appropriate, check in again to see if the purpose was met, and of course do so at the end of the investigation. Ask, "Why was setting a purpose helpful to our figuring things out? How was setting a purpose before reading a book the same or different from setting a purpose before doing a hands-on investigation?"

Figure 3.11 Sensemaking Strategies

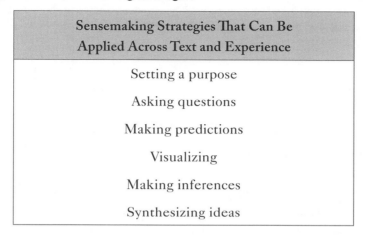

Sensemaking Strategies That Can Be Applied Across Text and Experience
Setting a purpose
Asking questions
Making predictions
Visualizing
Making inferences
Synthesizing ideas

Figure 3.12 "Setting Goals" class chart. Early on in a unit, the teacher sets the purpose or goal for investigation and reading.

Setting Goals	
Science Goals	Reading Goals
Figure out what magnets attract Find the resting position of a magnet hanging on a string	Find examples of forces Find evidence of forces Understand more about magnetic poles Understand the evidence that changed the scientists' explanation Learn more about what the words gravity and weight mean

Figure 3.13 *"Setting Goals" student sheet.* Over the course of a unit, students can take more responsibility in setting goals they have for investigation and reading. Here is a scaffolded version of a student sheet for grade 3 students.

Name _____ Date _____

Setting an Investigation Goal

Goal for the investigation:

Figure out

☑ if magnets can repel iron
☐ if both north and south poles of a magnet can attract iron
☐ if a magnet can attract iron through other materials

Our evidence:

When we hold a paper clip near a magnet, it is attracted to all parts of the magnet.

Our conclusion:

Both the north and south poles of a magnet attract iron.

Figure 3.14 **"Setting Goals" student sheet.** Here is a more open-ended version of a goal-setting student sheet for grade 5 students.

Name _____ Date _____

Reading with a Goal

How Big Is Big? How Far Is Far?

My reading goal:

find out how big Earth is

What did you learn about this reading goal?

Earth is not the largest planet in the Solar System.

Jupiter is much bigger than Earth.

There are over 200 countries on Earth.

Earth is big to us, but for a planet, it's pretty small.

- Periodically stop over the course of your class investigation to take stock of what the students have figured out so far and how they have figured it out. Ask, "What evidence did we get from reading/looking in this book? What evidence did we get from the experiment we did today? Thinking about all the information we have gathered, what claim can we make?"

Ask yourself: How am I supporting students in synthesizing information from multiple sources?

- When students present their explanations for phenomena, have them indicate where they got their evidence. You can provide a page with a graphic organizer that invites students to list the different evidence they have gathered, from which sources, and how that supports their new understanding.

Speaking and Writing Like a Scientist

Science knowledge is socially constructed. It grows out of negotiated meaning, where one research group puts forth a claim with evidence, another may find new evidence and elaborate on the claim or may interpret the same evidence differently, and so on. Engaging students in scientific ways of communicating through talk offers students these same opportunities to develop and refine their understanding and to share their results. Knowing the answer in your mind is not the same as being able to articulate the answer as a scientific explanation. Students need help to be able to turn their understanding into words, as a scientist would. Here are some suggestions for explicit instruction in how to help students engage in constructing both oral and written scientific explanations and to critique explanations as they engage in scientific argumentation.

What Makes an Explanation a Scientific Explanation?

Students' first encounter with a scientific explanation should focus them on the essential core of an explanation—that it answers a question

Figure 3.15a and b Synthesizing ideas from multiple sources. Help students organize and synthesize their thoughts by providing graphic organizers like these. Both of these are used with grade 5 students.

Name: _____ Date: _____

Synthesizing Ideas About Water Shortages

1. Read the question below.
2. Recall big ideas from *Water Encyclopedia* that help you answer the question, and record them in the first box.
3. Read pages 4–7 of *Water Shortages, Water Solutions* and record big ideas that help you answer the question in the second box.
4. Connect ideas together to come up with a new understanding that answers the question.
5. Record your new understanding in the box below the arrow.

Question: How can people affect how much freshwater is available?

Source: *Water Encyclopedia*

Ideas: Most of Earth's water is salt water, so there is not a lot of freshwater on Earth.

Source: *Water Shortages, Water Solutions*

Ideas: Overuse, drought, and pollution can lead to water shortages; When people use water, there is less clean freshwater available; When people use water, the amount of freshwater in reservoirs or lakes goes down.

↓

New understanding:
People affect how much freshwater is available when they use water. There is not very much freshwater on Earth, and if people use too much or pollute it, there is even less clean freshwater available.

The Earth System—Lesson 1.2

Incorporating Literacy Practices That Are Authentic to Science **83**

Name: _____ Date: _____

Synthesizing Ideas About Why Scientists Argue

1. Read the question below and think about what you read in *Why Do Scientists Argue?* as well as your experience making scientific arguments.
2. In each box, record important ideas related to the question. (You can write more than one idea in each box.)
3. In the box below the arrow, record a new understanding you have, based on thinking about the ideas together.

Question: How do scientists convince others that their claims are correct?

Source: *Why Do Scientists Argue?* (pages about scientists today) Ideas: They talk about their investigations. They use evidence to support their claims. They try to get more evidence when they disagree.
Source: *Why Do Scientists Argue?* (pages about Rachel Carson) Ideas: She collected lots of evidence about pesticides. She looked at data that other scientists collected. She wrote a book and talked a lot about her ideas.
Source: My experience as an ecologist making arguments Ideas: We use data from the project area. We get evidence from the Simulation and other sources. We talk about the evidence. We write arguments.

↓

New understanding: Scientists convince others that claims are correct by supporting those claims with evidence.

Ecosystem Restoration—Lesson 2.6

about how or why something happens. Because you are asking your students to explain something in science class, their explanations will automatically be focused on explaining phenomena from the natural world—an important characteristic of scientific explanations. Over time, you will want to provide students with more and more characteristics about scientific explanations, so they deepen their knowledge and understanding. Here are possible characteristics to share.

Checklist for a Scientific Explanation

- ☐ It answers a question about how or why something in the natural world happens.
- ☐ It describes things that are not easy to observe.
- ☐ It is based on the ideas you have learned from investigations and text.
- ☐ It uses scientific language.
- ☐ It is written for an audience.

Claim: a proposed answer to a question
Prediction: a tentative claim about how or why something happens
Scientific explanation: a claim about how or why something happens
Argument: a case made using evidence to show how a particular claim is the best one

Groundwork for Oral Explanations: Infuse Talk Opportunities

What follows are suggestions for providing productive student-to-student talk opportunities:

- Turn-and-talk. Probably the easiest to implement with frequency, the turn-and-talk routine is as simple as it sounds. Providing students with a prompt to discuss and ensuring that both students get a chance to talk—and recognize the importance of listening—can increase the productivity of this routine.
- Shared listening. Another productive talk routine is to provide pairs of students with a question. Partner A talks for 1–2 minutes uninterrupted, in response to the prompt. Partner A can use the following sentence starter: I think_____. Then Partner B

repeats back to Partner A what she heard Partner A say. Partner B can use this sentence starter: I heard you say_____. Follow this with a whole-class share-out, in which students share what their partner said.

- Practice explaining phenomena. Have students practice explaining how or why phenomena work. Assign pairs to talk through their initial explanations. First prompt them each to give a one-sentence answer to the question. Invite several pairs to share out and comment on these short answers/claims. Then have them each elaborate on their initial claims by describing more about how or why something happens. Again, have several pairs share out and comment on their elaborated explanations.

- Revisit prior understandings. You can scaffold students in connecting their new understanding to the predictions they made and facilitate the process of identifying what they have figured out. If you started a "What We Think We Know About X" class chart before the investigation (see page 55), now would be the time to revisit this chart. You can also begin a class chart now, or just orally review what students knew before investigating. Help them summarize what new information they have figured out by saying something like, "We have been figuring out a lot of different things about why the raisins floated, then sank, then floated again. Who can think of one thing we've figured out?"

- Roundtable discussions. Groups of four students discuss four related questions. Each student is responsible for acting as a discussion leader on one question. For that question, the student: (1) poses the question, (2) elicits response from the group, (3) makes sure all other group members contribute, and (4) takes notes about the group's ideas for that question. The discussion leader is also responsible for reporting on the group's ideas to the whole class in a debrief that takes place after the small-group discussions.

Figure 3.16 **Roundtable discussion.** Roundtable discussions offer students a low-stakes opportunity to express their thinking.

Name _____   Date _____

Roundtable Discussion: The Moon

Circle the number of the question below that you were assigned. (You will be the discussion leader for the question you circled.)

1. Where does the light we see from the Moon come from?

2. Can the Moon be seen in the daytime?

3. When the Moon is full, can you see it all night?

4. Does the Moon ever rise in the morning?

As your group discusses your question, take notes here:

Lunar Phase Simulator – full Moon overhead at midnight

Observing the Moon – observed full Moon at night

Moon Spheres – could see whole side of Moon lit

_____

_____

Questions to Ask Your Group
- What do you think?
- Why do you think that?
- What is your evidence?
- What does the evidence tell us?

Scientific Argument: Creating a Culture of Discourse

When we explicitly value, model, and provide opportunities for students to practice taking on a critical stance, we help them engage in thinking and talking like scientists. Scientific argumentation is a key science practice that is rooted in a culture of critique and contributes to rigorous standards for the establishment of knowledge. It is also a key literacy practice that enables students to communicate orally and in writing as a scientist would.

Students of all ages are actually quite good at mustering an oral argument—ask their families! This is a foundation on which you can build as students adopt the evidence-based approach that scientists bring to argumentation. Evidence-based argumentation should start in the earliest grades as students learn how scientists think and come to figure things out about the natural world.

Just as students need time and experience to come to understand what makes an explanation scientific, they also need time and experience to understand what makes an argument scientific. Here is a collection of characteristics of a scientific argument, which, like the characteristics of scientific explanations, can build gradually over the course of several years.

Checklist for a Scientific Argument

- ☐ It answers a question with a claim about the natural world.
- ☐ It includes evidence to support the claim. Evidence can be:
  - data collected by you or a trusted scientist
  - ideas from investigations
  - ideas from books
- ☐ It connects the evidence to the claim by linking different pieces of evidence together to show how they support the claim.
- ☐ It is written for an audience.
- ☐ It uses scientific language.
- ☐ It ends with a conclusion.

Following are some suggested structured discourse routines that support students in engaging in respectful, evidence-based argument:

- Evidence circles. Groups of four students discuss the relevance of evidence. Provide each group with a claim and each student with a piece of evidence. Have them take turns saying whether they think their piece of evidence is relevant to the claim or not. After each partner says what he or she thinks, other partners can add their ideas. They can go around again, this second time to say whether they think their piece of evidence supports the claim or not.

Figure 3.17 Evidence circles. Evidence circles are great ways for students to vet evidence before they begin writing an argument.

Name: _____ Date: _____

Evidence Circles: Desert Rocks National Park Environment

1. Read the question and the claim below.
2. Read each Evidence Card carefully. (You may want to take turns reading the cards aloud with your group.) Make notes below if you want to.
3. Talk about the evidence that supports the claim. Try to connect related data and ideas together.
4. See if all group members can come to agreement on whether the claim is supported by the evidence.
5. If there is no agreement, discuss the reasons your group still disagrees.

Question: What was the environment of Desert Rocks National Park like in the past?

Claim: Desert Rocks National Park used to be underwater.

Notes:

_____

_____

_____

_____

_____

_____

Earth's Features—Lesson 1.6

- Discourse circles. Groups of four students agree or disagree with a claim. Have pairs of students prepare for a discourse circle by gathering their ideas for and against a specific claim. Assemble groups of students with alternative views. Invite one person to share his or her position and evidence. Other students who agree add their evidence. Then a student who disagrees says why and presents his or her evidence. The group members discuss with one another to see if they can come to agreement. If they cannot agree, the group can talk about all the reasons why they are convinced of their own positions.

It takes time to build a classroom culture that encourages respect for all and makes honest, thoughtful critique possible. It also requires the communication of norms along with explicit valuing, modeling, and opportunities to practice what building ideas together looks like. Guide the class in using guidelines that include things like listen actively and share ideas, use evidence to justify ideas, disagree productively, and keep an open mind. Let students know that when scientists argue, they are not mad at each other; they are trying to come up with the best explanations for how the natural world works. As with other kinds of guidelines for classroom interactions, you might introduce the whole list at once but concentrate on one guideline at a time; introduce it to students guideline by guideline to create a growing list; or choose to have students generate a list over time (providing, of course, the necessary input, coaching, and experience before they are asked to articulate a particular guideline).

In class discussions during which students are sharing what they know and what they figured out, provide students with sentence frames for critiquing and for responding to critiques, such as: Why do you think that? What is your evidence? How could we be more sure? Help students who are struggling to respond by giving them the words to get started: I think that because . . . My evidence is . . . Make these questions and sentence starters visible in the classroom as anchor

Figure 3.18 Discourse circle. Here is a planning sheet students use prior to participating in a discourse circle.

Name _____   Date _____

Oil Spill Discourse Circle Response

Students like us CAN help prevent oil from spilling in the ocean.	
I agree with this statement. Here is my evidence.	I disagree with this statement. Here is my evidence.
We can use less oil and then so much oil won't have to be drilled and carried in ships that can have accidents.	We don't drive cars so we can't do anything about using lots of oil.
We can use less oil by walking instead of having our parents drive us places.	We can't tell people to get better oil tankers and be more careful so oil doesn't get spilled.
We can help prevent oil spills if we buy things with less plastic in the packages. Then less oil will be carried in the ships.	Adults don't listen to us when we tell them to recycle and use less oil.

charts, posted on sentence strips, or on personal bookmarks for each student. Provide positive feedback to students who take on a critical stance, querying each other and providing evidence-based responses.

Understanding that argument/critique is an evaluation of ideas, not of people, is key to understanding and treating argumentation as a constructive, collaborative activity. Find ways to communicate that scientists change their ideas when new evidence is uncovered, and students will be more likely to change theirs. You might describe times when scientists have changed their minds. A few examples follow:

- Scientists used to believe that birds are not intelligent. Now we have evidence that some birds, such as parrots and crows, are highly intelligent.
- Scientists used to believe that dinosaurs had green, scaly skin. New evidence has revealed that dinosaurs were more likely multicolored, and many were covered with feathers.
- Scientists used to believe that Neanderthals evolved into humans. There is now evidence that Neanderthals and humans overlapped in time and place, indicating that they were two different lines.

Modeling How to Write Explanations

Engaging in constructing oral explanations is a great way to start, but make sure not to assume that your students will know how to *write* a scientific explanation. You may choose to read some scientific explanations with students and discuss how they are constructed. Post a definition of a scientific explanation: it answers a question about how or why something happens. Model writing a scientific explanation. Think aloud as you write the topic sentence of your scientific explanation: "Let's see, the question we had was, Why do the raisins float, and then sink, and then float again in the ginger ale? What would the short answer to this question be? I'm going to say this: the bubbles of gas in the ginger ale cause the raisins to move up and down in the ginger ale. My short answer is my claim. OK, my claim is what I think is the answer to the question, but to be a good explanation it needs more details. I'm going to describe what happens in the order I observed. When you first put a raisin in the ginger ale, it sinks to the bottom of the liquid. Slowly, bubbles of gas in the ginger ale attach to the raisin. After enough bubbles have attached, the raisin begins to float upward toward the surface of the ginger ale. As more bubbles attach, the raisin floats higher in the liquid. When the bubbles that are attached to the raisin detach or pop, the raisin sinks lower in the liquid. As more bubbles attach, the raisin floats higher in the liquid again. This continues as long as there are bubbles in the ginger ale. The wrinkles on the raisin provide places for the bubbles to attach."

Depending on the age and experience of your students, you might want to write the first explanation together, getting input from the class as you write the explanation on the board. Alternatively, you can model writing a different scientific explanation and let students then write their own. Some teachers choose to provide a topic sentence for students the first time students create the explanation.

Being able to confidently write explanations requires having plenty of practice. Provide multiple opportunities for your students to write explanations, each time releasing more responsibility to them for writing or providing more support as needed.

Figure 3.19 shows several graphic organizers that can support students in gathering evidence and organizing their thinking before writing an explanation.

You may want to provide your students with a checklist to use as they create and then evaluate their explanations (see Figures 3.20 and 3.21).

Modeling How to Write Arguments

Simply stating an explanation (or claim) is not enough in science; scientists (and students) must justify that claim through argumentation. Post the definition of a scientific argument: providing evidence for why you think a claim (an explanation) is the best one. The same model-

Figures 3.19a, b, and c   Sample graphic organizers. Shown are several graphic organizers that can support students in gathering evidence and organizing their thinking before writing an explanation.

Name _____   Date _____

Gary's Mystery Sand

Record your observations and inferences in a table like Gary did in his sand journal.

1. Record your observations of the sand in column one.
2. Write your inferences about what that could be evidence of in column two.
3. Write your explanation.

Name of Sand: _Gary's Mystery Sand_____

	Observations	**Could be evidence of**
Size	small sand grains	came from beach with small waves
Shape	some are sharp and some are a little rounded	some grains are older and some are newer
Color	brown, orange, pink, black, white, purple	composed of shells

Explanation: _The sand grains are made from shells so there must be shelled animals living nearby. Waves broke the shells into small pieces and small waves brought them to the beach. I can tell that some shell pieces are not old because they are still colorful._

Graphic Organizer for a Scientific Explanation About Evaporation

Question: What can make evaporation happen faster?

water near the Sun
evaporated faster

higher
temperature

claim

higher temperatures, moving air, and low
humidity all make evaporation happen faster

**other ideas
from the
book**

puddles evaporate
faster on hot days than
on cold days

moving
air

low
humidity

water near a fan
evaporated faster

the droplets not covered
by the cup evaporated
faster than the
covered droplets

Name _____ **Date** _____

Planning a Scientific Explanation

Question: If you were on Jupiter, would Jupiter's moons have phases?

moons orbit Jupiter like the Moon orbits Earth	Jupiter rotates
Evidence	Evidence

Jupiter's moons have phases.

Claim

Jupiter's moons reflect light from the Sun	our Moon appears to change
Evidence	Evidence

Figure 3.20 This checklist was used after students had a lesson on using transition words and phrases.

Student Checklist for Scientific Explanations

Your name_____

Your partner's name_____

Check off each element in your partner's writing.

	Yes	No
1. Is there a claim?	✓	
2. Does the paragraph include evidence from the class investigations?	✓	
3. Does the paragraph include ideas from a book?	✓	
4. Does the paragraph use transition words or phrases?	✓	

Which ones? _for example, also, so_ _____

_____

Figure 3.21 Students in grade 4 were provided with two versions of the same scientific explanation: one using transition words and phrases, and the other not.

Scientific Explanation About Humidity

Question: Is humidity different in different places?

Example 1:

Humidity is different in different places. There was a lot of humidity near warm water in our classroom. It was more humid near a warm shower. We tested for humidity by the cool air near the fan. We did not find much. We tested for humidity near a cold wall in our classroom. There was not much humidity there. There is high humidity where it is warmer. There was more humidity near the shower and warm water and less near the fan and cold wall. Humidity is different in different places.

Example 2:

Humidity is different in different places. **For example**, there was a lot of humidity near warm water in our classroom. **We also found** that it was more humid near a warm shower. **Another** place we tested for humidity was the cool air near the fan, **but** we did not find much. **Finally**, we tested for humidity near a cold wall in our classroom. There was not much humidity there. There is high humidity where it is warmer, **so** this is why there was more humidity near the shower and warm water and less near the fan and cold wall. **All of these examples** show that humidity is different in different places.

Projection 2–1—Weather and Water 2.4

---

ing and think-aloud process we suggested for writing explanations can also scaffold the process of writing arguments. For instance, repost the explanation you wrote about how the floating raisins phenomenon works, and then model writing an argument: "We think this because we could actually see the bubbles of gas attaching to the raisins, and we could see the bubbles pop or come unattached right before the raisins sank again. We know that bubbles in ginger ale are filled with gas and that gases float in liquid. When enough bubbles attached to the raisin, the floating bubbles carried the raisin with them to the top of the liquid."

> **Ask yourself: How am I supporting students in writing explanations and arguments?**

The natural time to introduce written scientific argument is when there is a real reason to evaluate claims (explanations) to see which is the strongest—best supported by the evidence—and when there is a real audience to read and compare arguments. This opportunity will naturally occur after an investigation in which the class began with two claims and investigated to see which claim is best supported by the evidence. Students can make an argument for why their explanation (claim) is better than another. Invite pairs of students to trade their explanations and provide each other with feedback. Alternatively, you could write two different explanations and invite students to decide which one they agree with and why.

You can scaffold students' scientific argument writing in a variety of ways. For example, you can provide students with a graphic representation that invites them to write what their claim is and what evidence they have (data or ideas) that makes them feel confident in their claim. You may choose to have some things filled out for students, so they are just focusing on adding the argument to the explanation (see Figure 3.22). You could further scaffold the writing of the argument by having students record evidence they found (data from investigations or ideas from trusted science text) before turning those into sentences (see Figure 3.23). There is also a collection of free strategy guides that

Figure 3.22 Here is an example of how to scaffold students' writing an argument.

Name: _____ Date: _____

Rain Forest Restoration Plan 1

1. Write a scientific argument that answers the question below.
2. Include scientific ideas about what happened to the organisms and to the molecules.
3. Your audience is Natural Resources Rescue.
4. Your argument should include:
   - a claim that answers the question.
   - evidence that supports the claim, including
     - data from the project area.
     - ideas from Matter Makes It All Up .
     - ideas from the Simulation.

Question: Why aren't the jaguars and sloths growing and thriving?

The jaguars and sloths aren't growing and thriving because _____

_____.

The evidence shows that _____

_____

_____.

This matters because _____

_____

_____

_____.

This means that _____

_____

_____

_____.

Ecosystem Restoration—Lesson 1.8 (Version B)

Figure 3.23a and b You can further scaffold the writing of the argument by having students record evidence they found (data from investigations or ideas from trusted science texts) before turning those into sentences. Here are two examples, for grades 3 and 4, of mustering evidence in preparation for writing a scientific argument.

a

Name _____   Date _____

Gathering Evidence About Lenses and Light

Gather evidence to answer the question. Write the evidence in the correct box.

How do lenses interact with light?

Evidence of refraction:	Evidence of transmission:
saw light refracted through lens with tub of water, light bent	observed bright light spot on light detector
Evidence of reflection:	**Evidence of absorption:**
can see the lens small spot of light on light detector in front of lens	

Name _____ **Date** _____

Evidence That Air Is Something

Air takes up space.

We puffed up our cheeks with air and we filled the plastic
bag with air.

_____

_____

_____

_____

You can feel air.

We made the paper into a fan and made wind that we could
feel on our faces.

_____

_____

_____

_____

Air can move things.

We crumpled up some paper into little balls and blew at it
with the straw and it moved.

_____

_____

_____

_____

include activities that support students writing scientific explanations for middle school teachers at learningdesigngroup.org, developed by my team at the Lawrence Hall of Science. Our team also created the Argumentation Toolkit at argumentationtoolkit.org.

Helping Students Use Scientific Vocabulary

Scientists and engineers not only use highly precise and specific language, specialized to the domain, but they also use different language structures.

Figure 3.24   Scientific language. Some teachers post these sentence frames on the classroom wall as a reminder and support for what scientific argumentation sounds like.

Name: _____ Date: _____

Scientific Language for Evidence Circles

Ways to share ideas:

- I think _____ because _____.

- The evidence shows that _____.

- This idea is important because _____.

Ways to respond to others:

- I agree because _____.

- I disagree because _____.

Questions to ask during the discussion:

- What evidence supports the claim?

- Can you say more about why the evidence you shared supports the claim?

Earth's Features—Lesson 1.6

There are many ways to support students' acquisition of science vocabulary and science language.

- Select a small set of conceptually important words for extra attention in each science unit. The words should be central to the content learning goals for the unit. Thinking of words as simply labels for concepts can help you to focus on those words/concepts that are core to what the unit is about. Once you have selected these words, resist having an end-of-week quiz about their definitions and spelling. Instead, work to create multiple opportunities over the course of the entire unit for students to hear you using the words and for them to talk using the words, read the words, and write the words.

- Concept mapping allows students to graphically organize and represent their knowledge. One way is to start with a central word on the paper. Students can choose one of the class' core vocabulary words and show relationships between that concept and other concepts. This is typically done by drawing boxes around words and lines connecting the boxes. The goal is for students to begin to construct rich mental networks of concepts. Other variations are to start with a central question, or to create what are called propositional concept maps, which add language that connects the words in the boxes. See Figure 3.25 for examples.

- Semantic feature analysis is another form of concept mapping that lends itself to science content. In semantic features analysis, related ideas, activities, or phenomena are listed in column headers and features that are shared or different serve as row headings.

Figure 3.25a, b, c, and d   Sample concept maps. Here are several examples of concept maps.

a

How oil gets into the ocean

How to clean up spills

Oil Spills

The effects of spills

How to prevent spills

b

Name _____   Date _____

My Notes About Soil

Soil is brown or light brown. It can feel soft or hard or crunchy. Soil can smell good like a garden. Water soaks into soil. Roots grow through the soil and hold the plant in place.

_____

_____

_____

_____

Draw your own concept map.

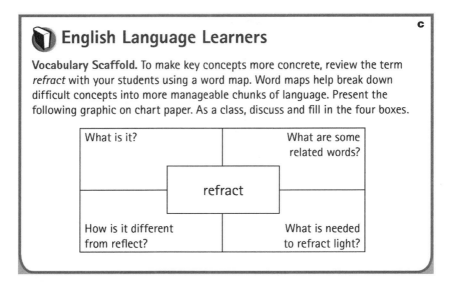

English Language Learners

Vocabulary Scaffold. To make key concepts more concrete, review the term *refract* with your students using a word map. Word maps help break down difficult concepts into more manageable chunks of language. Present the following graphic on chart paper. As a class, discuss and fill in the four boxes.

What is it?	What are some related words?
	refract
How is it different from reflect?	What is needed to refract light?

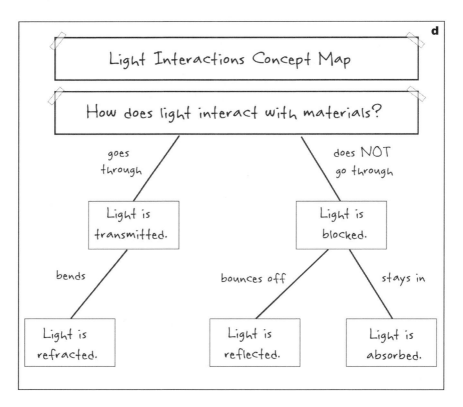

Light Interactions Concept Map

How does light interact with materials?

goes through — Light is transmitted.

does NOT go through — Light is blocked.

bends — Light is refracted.

bounces off — Light is reflected.

stays in — Light is absorbed.

Figure 3.26 Sample semantic feature map. Semantic feature analysis is another form of concept mapping.

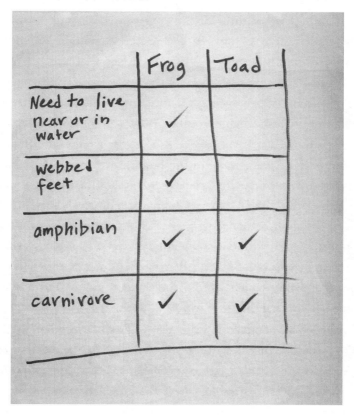

- A word relationships exercise can help students connect key vocabulary and concepts. Provide students with index cards, each with one of the core vocabulary words written on it. For example, in a grade 3 unit on balanced and unbalanced forces, you might select the following words: *force, balanced, unbalanced, exert, repel, attract, pole, object, gravity, evidence.* The first time you do this activity, limit the number you give students. In this case, you might choose three words: *force, exert, evidence.* Challenge pairs of students to first say a sentence that includes one of the words. They might say: "Gravity is an example of a force."

They can put the card with that word on it in front of them as they say the sentence. Then challenge them to say a sentence containing two or three of the core words, putting those cards in front of them as they say the sentence. Students might say: "When something moves, that is evidence that a force is being exerted." Next time you do this activity you might add *balanced* and *unbalanced*. The goal is for students to practice constructing sentences with the core vocabulary words and to explore ways in which the words are related as they try using more than one word in a sentence. One of the beauties of this activity is that there are many right answers, which reduces the pressure on students. Rather than having students write down these sentences, have them share orally with the whole class. This affords the opportunity for students to hear a variety of sentences utilizing the target vocabulary words. Engage students with the routine often, shifting which words students are given, and gradually increasing the number of words.

- Create a table connecting science-specific and everyday language. For instance, you can write the word *observe* on the chart and ask, "What is the everyday word for observe?" At students' prompting, write down words like *look*, *see*, and *notice*. Point out how observing involves using more than just the sense of sight, for example, hearing a noise or smelling an odor. Not one everyday word suffices to communicate that. That's why there is a specialized science word. Do this with other important words/concepts that come up. As students use an everyday language word, you can point to the chart and ask, "What's the science word for that?"

A great resource for innovative vocabulary instruction is the book *No More "Look Up the List" Vocabulary Instruction,* by Charlene Cobb and Camille Blachowicz (2014). There is also a collection of free science and literacy strategy guides that include ideas for vocabulary instruction for elementary students at scienceandliteracy.org.

Figure 3.27 **"Science/Everyday Word Chart."** Making an "Science/Everyday Word Chart" helps students learn precise science words to use in lieu of everyday language.

Science/Everyday Word Chart	
Science words	everyday words
observe	look, see, notice
record	write down
substance	ingredient, material
test	way to get evidence

There are different kinds of texts and reasons for reading texts in science and engineering than in other disciplines, and consequently scientists and engineers read text differently. Likewise, doing science involves synthesizing information from multiple sources, using different language, prioritizing a certain kind of evidence, and being able to construct explanations and arguments based on evidence. All these practices of the domain are things that need to be learned and, like other important science practices, benefit from explicit instruction. Following are a list of questions to help you provide these supports to your students as you teach.

Ask yourself: How am I supporting students in the use of scientific language?

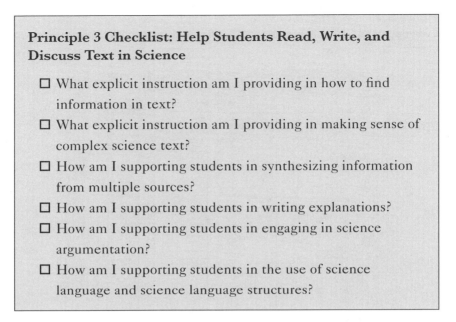

Principle 3 Checklist: Help Students Read, Write, and Discuss Text in Science

☐ What explicit instruction am I providing in how to find information in text?

☐ What explicit instruction am I providing in making sense of complex science text?

☐ How am I supporting students in synthesizing information from multiple sources?

☐ How am I supporting students in writing explanations?

☐ How am I supporting students in engaging in science argumentation?

☐ How am I supporting students in the use of science language and science language structures?

Just as the fields of science and engineering have evolved over time, so have expectations in the field for best practices in preparing students to be science literate. Stand-alone activities will not provide students with the opportunities to figure out the natural and designed worlds like scientists and engineers do. Rather, we want to see classrooms engaged in long instructional sequences, in which students learn about the natural world in the ways that scientists do, through firsthand experiences, experiences with physical and digital models, reading trusted science texts, using primary sources, writing explanations and arguments, and engaging in oral argumentation. The lovely thing is that students are quite capable of doing it all, and they thrive as they experience the power of using science to figure something out or engineering to solve a problem.

Figure 3.28 **"What Scientists Do" class chart.** Creating a class chart enables students to articulate what scientists do and how what the class did is similar.

What Scientists Do

Predictions about what scientists do	What scientists do	How we were like scientists
find answers	often work in groups	worked in groups
work in labs	ask questions	supported claims with evidence
invent things	read other scientists' work	made tables with data
know about light	when they disagree they look for more evidence	investigated questions
mix things together	support claims with evidence	changed our ideas about reflection
	revise ideas when they learn something new	got evidence from books

AFTERWORD
Nell K. Duke

Education often operates with *"or"* when it should be *"and."* For example, phonics instruction *or* immersing children in meaningful opportunities to read? *No*, phonics instruction *and* immersing children in meaningful opportunities to read. Hands-on science investigations *or* learning about science through reading? *No*, again, hands-on investigations *and* learning about science through reading, as Jacquey Barber and Gina Cervetti have so powerfully conveyed.

The instruction that Jacquey and Gina describe is seen all too rarely in practice. In fact, in many of the districts in which I work, there is virtually no science instruction of any kind happening in the early elementary grades. Even at the fourth-grade level, data from the National Assessment of Educational Progress 2015 found that more than one-fifth of teachers reported less than two hours a week of science instruction, and only a quarter reported what would amount to four or more hours a week (Change the Equation, based on the National Assessment of Educational Progress 4th-Grade Science Assessment 2015).

It is so difficult to find time for all that we are expected to teach, but I believe Jacquey and Gina have provided us with a way forward—a way to ensure that teaching science not only fosters development in science but also fosters development in literacy, and a way that teaching literacy not only fosters literacy but also fosters development in science. This is not an easy way forward, but it allows us to act upon some core beliefs.

- Children have the right to learn about the natural world.
- Children have the right to engage actively in the "doing" of science, not simply reading about science.
- Children have the right to read, write, and discuss in science—as professional scientists and citizen scientists do.

- Children have the right to instruction that helps them learn to read, write, and discuss science.
- Children have the right to use science, including literacy practices within science, to have an impact on the world around them.

I'm grateful for the guidance that Jacquey and Gina have provided for us to enact these rights using insights from research and from years of curriculum development and practice. I'm grateful to you for striving to enact these rights in your practice.

REFERENCES

ACT, Inc. 2006. *Reading Between the Lines: What the ACT Reveals About College Readiness in Reading.* Iowa City, IA: Authors.

Anderson, E. 1998. "Motivational and Cognitive Influences on Conceptual Knowledge: The Combination of Science Observation and Interesting Texts" (doctoral dissertation). College Park, MD: University of Maryland.

Banilower, E. R., P. S. Smith, K. A. Malzahn, C. L. Plumley, E. M. Gordon, and M. L. Hayes. 2018. Report of the 2018 NSSME +. Chapel Hill, NC: Horizon Research, Inc.

Barber, J. 2007. *Jess Makes Hair Gel.* Seeds of Science/Roots of Reading. University of California, Berkeley.

Barton, A. C., and E. Tan. 2010. "'We Be Burnin'!' Agency, Identity, and Science Learning." *Journal of the Learning Sciences* 19 (2): 187–229.

Beals, K., and P. D. Pearson. 2007. *Why Aren't Rain Boots Made of Paper?* Seeds of Science/Roots of Reading. University of California, Berkeley.

Belland, B. R., J. Gu, N. J. Kim, and D. J. Turner. 2016. "An Ethnomethodological Perspective on How Middle School Students Addressed a Water Quality Problem." *Educational Technology Research and Development* 64: 1135–61.

Berland, L. K., C. V. Schwarz, C. Krist, L. Kenyon, A. S. Lo, and B. J. Reiser. 2016. "Epistemologies in Practice: Making Scientific Practices Meaningful for Students." *Journal of Research in Science Teaching* 53: 1082–12.

Bill and Melinda Gates Foundation. 2010. *Fewer, Clearer, Higher.* www.gatesfoundation.org.

Bravo, M. A., and G. N. Cervetti. 2014. "Attending to the Language and Literacy Needs of English Learners in Science." *Equity & Excellence in Education* 47: 230–45.

Buck, G. A., K. L. Cook, C. F. Quigley, P. Prince, and Y. Lucas. 2014. "Seeking to Improve African American Girls' Attitudes Toward Science: A Participatory Action Research Project." *Elementary School Journal* 114: 431–53.

Burns, D. *Trees, Leaves, and Bark.* 1995. Take-Along Guide Series. Minnetonka, MN: North Word Books for Young Readers.

Cervetti, G. N., J. Barber, R. Dorph, P. D. Pearson, and P. Goldschmidt. 2012. "The Impact of an Integrated Approach to Science and Literacy in Elementary School Classrooms." *Journal of Research in Science Teaching* 49: 631–58.

Cervetti, G. N., A. DiPardo, and S. Staley. 2014. "Entering the Conversation: Exploratory Talk in Middle School Science." *The Elementary School Journal* 114: 547–72.

Cervetti, G. N., P. D. Pearson, J. Barber, E. Hiebert, and M. Bravo. 2007. "Integrating Literacy and Science: The Research We Have, the Research We Need." In *Shaping Literacy Achievement: Research We Have, Research We Need,* edited by M. Pressley, A. K. Billman, K. Perry, K. Refitt, and J. Reynolds, 157–74. New York: Guilford.

Cobb, C., C. Blachowisz. 2014. *No More "Look Up the List" Vocabulary Instruction.* Not This, But That Series. Portsmouth, NH: Heinemann.

Common Core State Standards Initiative. 2010. *Common Core State Standards.* Washington, DC: National Governors Association and the Council of Chief State School Officers.

Craig, M. T., and L. D. Yore. 1995. "Middle School Students' Metacognitive Knowledge About Science Reading and Science Text: An Interview Study." *Reading Psychology* 16: 169–213.

Dendy, L. *Tracks, Scats, and Signs.* 1995. Take-Along Guide Series. Minnetonka, MN: North Word Books for Young Readers.

Dorph, R., P. Shields, J. Tiffany-Morales, A. Hartry, and T. McCaffrey. 2011. *High Hopes–Few Opportunities: The Status of Elementary Science Education in California.* Sacramento, CA: The Center for the Future of Teaching and Learning at WestEd.

Duke, N., and V. Bennett-Armistead. 2003. *Reading and Writing Informational Text in the Primary Grades: Research-Based Practices.* New York: Scholastic.

Duke, N. K., G. N. Cervetti, and C. Wise. 2016. "The Teacher and the Classroom." (Special retrospective issue of *Journal of Education* on *Becoming a Nation of Readers.*) *Journal of Education* 196 (3): 35–43.

Ford, D. J. 2009. "Promises and Challenges for the Use of Adapted Primary Literature in Science Curricula: Commentary." *Research in Science Education* 39: 385–90.

Goldman, S. R., M. A. Britt, W. Brown, G. Cribb, G., M. George, M.C. Greenleaf, C. Lee, and C. Shanahan. 2016. "Disciplinary Literacies and Learning to Read for Understanding: A Conceptual Framework for Disciplinary Literacy." *Educational Psychologist* 51 (2): 219–46.

Guthrie, J. T., E. Anderson, S. Alao, and J. Rinehart. 1999. "Influences of Concept-Oriented Reading Instruction on Strategy Use and Conceptual Learning from Text." *The Elementary School Journal* 99: 343–66.

Guthrie, J. T., and K. E. Cox. 2001. "Classroom Conditions for Motivation and Engagement in Reading." *Educational Psychology Review* 13: 283–302.

Guthrie, J. T., L. W. Hoa, A. Wigfield, S. M. Tonks, and K. C. Perencevich. 2006. "From Spark to Fire: Can Situational Reading Interest Lead to Long-Term Reading Motivation?" *Reading Research and Instruction* 45: 91–117.

Guthrie, J. T., A. McRae, and S. L. Klauda. 2007. "Contributions of Concept-Oriented Reading Instruction to Knowledge About Interventions for Motivations in Reading." *Educational Psychologist* 42 (4): 237–50.

Guthrie, J. T., and A. Wigfield. 2000. "Engagement and Motivation in Reading." In *Handbook of Reading Research: Volume III*, edited by M. L. Kamil, P. B. Mosenthal, P. D. Pearson, and R. Barr, 403–22. New York: Erlbaum.

Guthrie, J. T., A. Wigfield, P. Barbosa, K. C. Perencevich, A. Taboada, M. H. Davis, N. T. Scafiddi, and S. Tonks. 2004. "Increasing Reading Comprehension and Engagement Through Concept-Oriented Reading Instruction." *Journal of Educational Psychology* 96: 403–23.

Hines, P. J., B. Wible, and M. McCartney. 2010. "Science, Language, and Literacy: Learning to Read, Reading to Learn." *Science* 328: 447.

Holliday, W. G., L. D. Yore, and D. E. Alvermann. 1994. "The Reading-Science Learning Writing Connection: Breakthroughs, Barriers, and Promises." *Journal of Research in Science Teaching* 31: 877–94.

Kang, J., and T. Keinonen. 2018. "The Effect of Student-Centered Approaches on Students' Interest and Achievement in Science: Relevant Topic-Based, Open and Guided Inquiry-Based, and Discussion-Based Approaches." *Research in Science Education* 48 (4): 865–85.

Magnusson, S., and A. S. Palincsar. 2004. "Learning from Text Designed to Model Scientific Thinking in Inquiry-Based Instruction." In *Crossing Borders: Connecting Science and Literacy*, edited by W. Saul. Newark, DE: International Reading Association.

McKeown, M. G., I. L. Beck, and R. G. K. Blake. 2009. "Rethinking Reading Comprehension Instruction: A Comparison of Instruction for Strategies and Content Approaches." *Reading Research Quarterly* 44: 218–53.

Moje, E. B. 2008. "Foregrounding the Disciplines in Secondary Literacy Teaching and Learning: A Call for Change." *Journal of Adolescent and Adult Literacy* 52: 96–107.

Moore. D. W., J. E. Readence, and R. J. Rickelman. 1983. "An Historical Exploration of Content Area Reading Instruction." *Reading Research Quarterly* 18: 419–38.

National Research Council. 2012. *A Framework for K–12 Science Education: Practices, Crosscutting Concepts, and Core Ideas.* Washington, DC: The National Academies Press.

Palincsar, A. S. 2005. *Reading in Science: Why, What, and How* (Brief). Washington, DC: National Science Resources Center.

Parizeau, N. 2007. *The Black Tide*, Seeds of Science/Roots of Reading. University of California, Berkeley.

Potvin, P., and A. Hasni. 2014. "Interest, Motivation and Attitude Toward Science and Technology at K–12 Levels: A Systematic Review of 12 Years of Educational Research." *Studies in Science Education* 50: 85–129.

Purcell-Gates, V., N. K. Duke, and J. A. Martineau. 2007. "Learning to Read and Write Genre-Specific Text: Roles of Authentic Experience and Explicit Teaching." *Reading Research Quarterly* 42: 8–45.

RAND Reading Study Group. 2002. *Reading for Understanding.* Santa Monica, CA: RAND.

Romance, N. R., and M. R. Vitale. 1992. "A Curriculum Strategy That Expands Time for In-Depth Elementary Science Instruction by Using Science-Based Reading Strategies: Effects of a Year-Long Study in Grade Four." *Journal of Research in Science Teaching* 29: 545–54.

———. 2001. "Implementing an In-Depth Expanded Science Model in Elementary Schools: Multi-Year Findings, Research Issues, and Policy Implications." *International Journal of Science Education* 23: 373–404.

————. 2011. "A Research-Based Instructional Model for Integrating Meaningful Learning in Elementary Science and Reading Comprehension: Implications for Policy and Practice." In *Developmental Cognitive Science Goes to School*, edited by N. L. Stein and S. W. Raudenbush, 127–42. New York: Routledge.

Rothman, Robert 2013. *Fewer, Clearer, Higher: How the Common Core State Standards Can Change Classroom Practice*. Cambridge, MA: Harvard Education Press.

Shanahan, C., T. Shanahan, and C. Misischia. 2011. "Analysis of Expert Readers in Three Disciplines: History, Mathematics, and Chemistry." *Journal of Literacy Research* 43: 393–429.

Silver, D., and P. Wynne. 1997. One Small Square series. Boston, MA: McGraw-Hill Education

Slavin, R. E., C. Lake, P. Hanley, and A. Thurston. 2014. "Experimental Evaluations of Elementary Science Programs: A Best-Evidence Synthesis." *Journal of Research in Science Teaching* 51: 870–901.

Smithsonian. 1992. The Smithsonian Handbooks. New York: Dorling-Kindersley, Inc.

Strack, E., and G. Plantevin, *What's the Difference?* 2018. San Francisco, CA: Chronicle Books, LLC.

Swan, E. A. 2003. *Concept-Oriented Reading Instruction: Engaging Classrooms, Lifelong Learners*. New York: Guilford Press.

University of California, Berkeley. 2014. Seeds of Science/Roots of Reading curricular program. Amplify Education, Inc. https://seedsofsciencerootsofreading .wordpress.com

Vitale, M. R., and N. R. Romance. 2012. "Using In-Depth Science Instruction to Accelerate Student Achievement in Science and Reading Comprehension in Grades 1–2." *International Journal of Science and Mathematics Education* 10: 457–72.

Wang, J., and J. Herman. 2005. *Evaluation of Seeds of Science/Roots of Reading Project: Shoreline Science and Terrarium Investigations*. Los Angeles, CA: CRESST.

Weiss, I. R., E. R. Banilower, K. C. McMahon, and P. S. Smith. 2001. *Report of the 2000 National Survey of Science and Mathematics Education*. Chapel Hill, NC: Horizon Research, Inc.

Yore, L. D., G. L. Bisanz, and B. M. Hand. 2003. "Examining the Literacy Component of Science Literacy: 25 Years of Language Arts and Science Research." *International Journal of Science Education* 25: 689–725.